Acclaim for

✦ *More and more people use Googlicious reveals how yo. ... business to the next level.*
— Perry Belcher, Top Internet Marketer, www.perrybelcher.com

✦ *If you are suffering from internet-phobia, you will be cured after reading this book. Be empowered as a real guerrilla to use these internet marketing weapons.*
—Jay Conrad Levinson, The Father of Guerrilla Marketing

✦ *Shamayah has a gift! This is one of the most practical, hands-on books you will find. What's more, the results you'll see for your business will be mind-blowing.*
—Stefanie Hartman, Profit Consultant & International Speaker, www.StefanieHartman.com

✦ *Your results will be exponential when you implement the right Internet marketing strategies. There is no need to waste time and money figuring it out by yourself. Take the fast track and let the experts of Googlicious help you. The sooner you start, the better.*
—Wyatt Knight, CEO of Eagle Asset Resolutions, www.earllc.com

✦ *The Internet offers great opportunities for business owners to transform their lives. Follow the formula in Googlicious to make money online and turn your computer into a cash machine!*
—Tom Antion, Top Internet Marketer, www.greatinternetmarketingtraining.com

✦ *In our information overload society it is key to have a sizzling online strategy. This is why Googlicious is a must read for every business owner. Learn how to create a laser-focused strategy to reach your online market so that you can drive sales and results for your business TODAY!*
—David Asarnow, The Peak Performance Strategist, www.DavidAsarnow.com

✦ *Googlicious will open your eyes to an online world of possibilities you didn't even know existed.*
—Stacey Dougan, Vegan & Raw Food Chef, www.staceydougan.com

✦ *Learn the power of information and joint ventures written in John C. Robinson's gentle yet focused and informative style. He is a true gem, sharing his knowledge to release your business ideas as if by magic.*
—PaTrisha-Anne Todd, LCSi, Ambassador for Success and Prosperity, www.cosmic-soul-coaching.com

✦ *Googlicious is a great collection of concisely presented knowledge and advice from industry experts. It is content rich, yet the format is easily digestible. This book is a must have—Googlicious can make you money!!!*
— Matthew Finkelstein, Personal Excellence & Prosperity Expert, www.mattfinkelstein.com

✦ *The world is changing and you can't stay behind. Just like I had to learn how to send text messages, because it's the best way to communicate with my grandchildren, you need to connect with your customers online. Googlicious will teach you exactly how.*
— Minnie Byers, The Streetwise Sales Expert

✦ *Googlicious is an incredible book! We can't deny that the Internet plays a critical role in business success today. Your strategy will become crystal clear after reading this book!*
— Jordan Adler, Top distributor Send Out Cards, Author of *Beach Money*, www.beachmoney.com.

✦ *As a professor at Rutgers University having had a 30 year career in marketing and business management (the last of which of as a professor), I can attest to the fact that the principles in this book are well founded and true for those that are willing to learn and apply them. You will benefit greatly!*
— Myron Finkelstein, Acting Director of Sports Studies Program at Rutgers University

✦ *Enjoy the clear and carefully presented information in this book! Without a doubt you'll find personal value and great ideas for your business.*
— Tracie Church, The Master Entrepreneurial Administrative Implementer, Experience Assistance with TLC

✦ *As a solopreneur it can be a challenge to figure the online stuff out. You know it's important, but where do you start? Thanks to Shamayah and the other experts I have much more clarity and know exactly how to grow my business using the Internet.*
— Bonny Lin, www.blisslightwellness.com

✦ *Inspirational and powerful! Shamayah gives you the roadmap to enhance your life and business, whether you are an entrepreneur, an author, or a speaker.*
— Rick Frishman, Morgan James Publishing

GOOGLICIOUS

The Internet Marketing Secrets
Every Business Should Use

**Shamayah Sarrucco
and Coauthors**

Foreword by Loral Langemeier

LiveOutLoud Publishing

Googlicious

The Internet Marketing Secrets Every Business Should Use
Copyright © 2011 by Shamayah Sarrucco

For information, or to order additional
copies of this book, please contact:

Live Out Loud Publishing
Phone: 707-688-2848 | Fax: 707-402-6319
Email: **info@earnprofitsfromyourpassion.com**

Cover and book design by Cypress House

Publisher's Cataloging-in-Publication Data

Sarrucco, Shamayah.
    Googlicious : the Internet marketing secrets every business should use / Shamayah Sarrucco and co-authors ; foreword by Loral Langemeier. -- 1st ed. -- Marysville, OH : Live Out Loud Pub., c2010.
    p. ; cm.
    ISBN: 978-0-9679338-4-9
    Includes "Googlicious" resources.
    1. Internet marketing. 2. Internet advertising. 3. Web sites-- Design. 4. Business enterprises--Automation. 5. Customer relations--Technological innovations. 6. Electronic commerce. I. Title.
    HF5415.1265 .S27 2010 2010911798   658.8/72028546-- dc22 1012

Printed in the USA
2 4 6 8 9 7 5 3 1
First edition

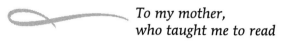 *To my mother,*
who taught me to read

This is the beginning of a new day.
God has given me this day to use as I will.
I can waste it or use it for good.
What I do today is very important,
Because I am exchanging a day of my life for it.
When tomorrow comes, this day will be gone forever,
Leaving something in its place I have traded for it.
I want it to be a gain, not loss—good, not evil.
Success, not failure, in order that I shall not forget the price
I paid for it.

— *Poem found in Paul "Bear" Bryant's Wallet*

 # Contents

 # Acknowledgments

I want to express my deepest gratitude...

To the people who have contributed to the idea and realization of this book as well as the support needed to complete it. Most of all I want to thank my creator, Jehovah God, for the talent and opportunity He has given me to grow, to set myself free of my past, and to live my true self.

To my dear mom, who has cultivated in me the love for books and the determination never to give up on my dreams. *Thank you, Mom, for believing in me and for your never-ending support.*

To Tanya, Elmy, Terya, and Sharryl, the most fabulous sisters in the world, for their love, friendship, and encouragement.

To my dear friends, Mikel Jones, who encouraged and helped me in so many ways; and John Gration — *Thank you for bringing the writer out in me, John.*

To each one of the great authors who contributed their knowledge and expertise that make this book so valuable.

To Loral Langemeier and her team, especially John C. Robinson. Their support was incredible.

To my family, especially Uncle Fred, Aunt Thecla, my cousin Gerda Keijzer, and her husband Gino.

To all the friends and special people who touched my life—Minnie and Jim Byers, Otis Boone, Winette Zichterman, Daniel Dirk Kooiman, Jan de Blanken, Ferry Doppenbecker, Carine Masaki, Lestrez Masaki, Virgenie Masaki, Aneissa van Metre, Andrea Doggett, David Asarnow, Leon Meir, Robert Benninga, and Molly Maxey.

To my amazing Master Mind group, Rhonda Anderson, Wyatt Knight, and Danny Lilly: our weekly calls continue to be an inspiration as they ignite even better ideas.

To the special people who empowered me when I needed it most:

—*Toine Revier, I'll always be grateful for the difference you have made in my life. Thank you so much.*

—*Brandon Bays, thank you for introducing "The Journey" to the world.*

—*Hannelieke Vorsterman, thank you for your friendship.*

To you, our reader, for your trust and your desire to make your life and business even better!

 # Foreword

Entrepreneurs throughout history have been the backbone of our economy. We are the innovators, doers, creators, generators, and expanders. We employ more than half of this country's workers. Small business is almost always responsible for converting a downturn into an upswing. It's time we all get involved because we're at the brink of an amazing period and opportunities are abundant. All you need is the right information and the tools to get there.

If you haven't caught on by now to the Internet's newest "big" thing, you must have been living under a rock. In a world of what's hot and what's not, the social media boom is smokin'! Facebook continues to add about 200,000 users a day, Twitter grew by 422% in 2008 alone, and LinkedIn has grown by 319% since 2007. Internet advertising, unlike "traditional marketing," is up 21% in spite of the economic downturn.

Do you know how to effectively use Facebook and Twitter for your business? With the economy in its current condition, being creative with advertising dollars is as important as staying current with marketing trends. This not-so-new trend will prove to be a saving grace for those with little to no advertising budget. Businesses of all sizes are jumping on this wave and riding it all the way to the bank.

We all want to connect, interact, and make friends. We all want to feel that we belong. That is what makes social media so powerful, but if you don't know the right way to use it, you will push people away. Nobody likes to be sold to, yet we all like to buy when we feel we're getting a good deal. This means you have to have value (content) when you talk to your on-line "friends." Frank Kern, one of the top Internet marketers and a self-made millionaire, uses this technique to make clients come to him asking if they can buy. He's brought in $23.8 million in just 24 hours!

Learning new Internet marketing techniques can be a hard transition for some. Most entrepreneurs fall in love with their business, often losing focus on creating new money. That's natural, but don't let that hold you back from expanding your social media community and in turn, your business. It can be that you don't know how to get started or you may not feel you have the time to do it all. Either way, don't worry, just continue reading. Learning how to use social media marketing may seem out of reach to you, but it's there and all you need to do is get started. *Googlicious* will show you the way.

Shamayah Sarrucco, John C. Robinson, and the team from my Loral's Big Table community have done a great job in creating *Googlicious*. This book provides busy business owners all the necessary tools in one place, in a clear and concise way.

It's time to wake up, get off the couch and start moving. I challenge you today to step up and move forward with your marketing strategies. Read *Googlicious* and get into action now!

Loral Langemeier, Founder/CEO of LiveOutLoud.com, best-selling author of the *Millionaire Maker* three-book series and *Put More Cash In Your Pocket*, money expert, and international speaker.

# Introduction
are you living by
design or by default?

*One day a father came home late from work. He was tired and ir-
ritated when he found his six-year-old son waiting for him at the
door. The little boy hugged his dad and said, "Daddy, may I ask
you a question?"*

*"Of course," his father answered. "What is it you would like to
ask?"*

"Daddy, how much money do you make an hour?"

*The father was shocked. "That is none of your business, my son!"
he replied.*

*"Please tell me, dad, how much money do you make an hour? I
really need to know," the little boy insisted.*

*"Well, if you must know, I make one hundred dollars per hour,"
his father answered, irritated.*

*"Oh," the little boy replied, disappointed. Then, apparently excited
by a new idea, he asked, "Can I please borrow fifty dollars, dad?"*

*Now his father started to get angry. "If the only reason you ask
me how much money I make is because you want to borrow money
for some silly thing, you better go straight to bed. I have had a long
day and am exhausted. Why are you being so selfish?"*

*The boy quietly went to his room and shut the door. The father
sat down and started to get even angrier about his son's questions.
How dare he ask such questions only to get some money? After a
while he calmed down and started to think: his son didn't ask for*

money very often — maybe he really needed the $50.

He went upstairs and knocked on his son's door, asking, "Are you awake?" He walked into the room and as his son had not yet fallen asleep, he gave the boy a hug and said, "I'm sorry I wasn't nice to you earlier. Business isn't going well and I have worked so many hours. Here is the fifty dollars you asked for."

The little boy got up with a big smile on his face. "Oh, thank you, Daddy!" he yelled. Then he reached in a jar where he pulled out some crumpled up bills and started counting the money.

His father's temper began to rise again. "Why did you ask me for fifty dollars, if you already had money?" he asked.

The little boy looked up at his father and answered, "Because I didn't have enough, but now I do. Daddy, I have one hundred dollars. Can I buy an hour of your time? Can you please come home early tomorrow? I would like to have dinner with you."

The father was crushed. He put his arms around his little son, and begged for his forgiveness.

Could this be you? Could it be your son, your daughter, or maybe your husband or wife who wants to buy an hour of your time? One day, when you are old and gray, you will be sitting at your favorite chair next to the window looking back on your life. What will you say to yourself?

Will you express happiness over the choices you made and say things like "I am glad I did ... "? Or, will you regret the years you've spent thinking, "I wish I had ..."? If we don't pay attention, we can get so caught up in everything we have to do that we forget what is really important. Before we know it, another day, another week, or even another month goes by and suddenly another year has passed.

> We can make a living
> or design a life.
>
> — *Jim Rohn*

Everybody has twenty-four hours in a day and we can only do so much. We are limited in the time we can spend to make money. If you are a business owner, you may perceive there are geographic limitations to the number of customers you can reach. The Internet provides the opportunity to overcome these limitations and has opened up doors to new possibilities that allow us to create leverage.

You see, my vision was to build a business allowing me to travel and live wherever I want in the world. In the last year alone I have been skiing in France, saw the great architecture in Chicago, experienced the beauty of the Rocky Mountains, visited "Garden of the Gods" in Colorado Springs, rode a bike along the canals in Amsterdam, ate Belgian waffles in Brussels, went on a boat to see the spectacular Niagara Falls up close, walked the fascinating streets of New York, surfed the waves in gorgeous Costa Rica, and took pictures of beautiful Lake Tahoe. I have lived in Amsterdam (the Netherlands), Montclair (New Jersey), and in Las Vegas (Nevada). Thanks to the Internet I can live and work where life is fun! Even if your business doesn't allow you this level of freedom, you can still benefit from the leverage the Internet can give you. "But," you may ask, "where do I start?"

Figuring out how to use the Internet for your business can be overwhelming at times. At least that was my experience when I first started. There is so much to learn! When I realized there were so many business owners around me who were struggling to figure it out, I decided to select fifteen experts in their fields to share their secrets of Internet marketing. I am excited to share these with you and help you in living your life by design.

Let's face it, when is the last time you used the Yellow Pages to find a restaurant, a store, or anything else you were looking for? If you are like most people, you probably can't even remember. Where do you look for a phone number, a new computer, or a recipe? Yep! Online! Well, you are not the only one. Your potential clients also go online to search for what they need or to resolve a problem. The question is, *Can they find you?* This book is filled with valuable information you can apply to help more clients find you using search engine optimization and social media. I will introduce you to Kathy Alice Brown, who will explain how to create or redesign your website so you will get better results; and to John Limbocker, who is an expert in getting more people to your site.

Maybe you have seen a sign at the cashier or a link on your competitor's website saying, "Follow us on Twitter." Or, maybe you have heard your clients talk about Facebook, making you wonder if you should use social media. If so, you have to meet Meredith Collins and Terza Ekholm, because they will show you how to get started. Especially in the current economical stormy times, you need to set up all sails to make it safely through the storm and be successful. Capitalizing on the possibilities the Internet offers is a very strong sail. The world is changing and developing at such a fast pace, you can't afford to stay behind.

It may seem that technology is taking over our society; in reality human nature is the same as it always has been. We are social beings — we want to connect, interact, make friends, feel we belong, are appreciated and valued. This won't change. Nohra Leff does a great job explaining the power of video marketing. Videos make your clients feel more connected to you. When you read her chapter, you will very likely agree video marketing has to be part of your business.

The basic success principle is to build relationships. Every successful person can tell you how networking and connecting with the right people at the right time are crucial for your success. At first it may seem cold and abstract to network from your computer, but Jacqueline McCarthy will help you realize you can really build valuable relationships online. She makes it clear the same principles we use in everyday life apply online; it is just a different forum.

> People don't want to be "marketed to,"
> They want to be "communicated with."
> — *Flint McGlaughlin*

The cool part is, you don't have to do it all on your own. As small business owners we tend to do everything ourselves. Once you understand the Internet Marketing Secrets we are sharing with you in this book, you can lead a team to help you execute your online strategy. Peter and Dianne Ivett describe in chapter 15 how to build a team successfully. And if are you one of those entrepreneurs who can't take a break, who is on vacation and still on the phone constantly, you can absolutely benefit from having a Virtual Assistant like Janice E. Clements (chapter 14).

Thank you and congratulations for picking up this awesome book! There is a reason you are reading this: "When the student is ready, the teacher appears." Are you ready to take your business and your life to the next level? Are you ready to play bigger and start living by design instead of by default? I am excited to share the following "teachers" with you, so you can make that happen. Don't allow precious time to slip through your fingers instead of spending it with those closest to your heart. Time is the most precious commodity; because once it's gone it can never be replaced.

Write your way to wealth

Shamayah Sarrucco

While sitting on a beautiful white beach in Costa Rica drinking a delicious fruit smoothie, I was watching the waves crash along the shore. Samara Beach was quiet that time of the year, making it very peaceful. At the seminars I had attended the last few years successful business owners seemed to have a common theme:"Do what you love and the money will follow." I took a sip from my smoothie. It puzzled me. Like most people I had always picked a job or a business, because of the money it would generate, not because I really enjoyed doing it. As I had been so focused on making money, I had a hard time figuring out what I would love to do.

The sun was about to set, giving the sky the most fabulous collection of colors. There I was, watching the most amazing sunset, contemplating what my passion was, when it suddenly hit me—I love to write and I love to organize! This is what I have enjoyed doing ever since I was a kid. Now the next question was, "How do I build a business from my passion?" I didn't want to be a journalist or write for a magazine. I gave it some more thought, but I couldn't come up with a business model that would allow me to write and organize. It was starting to get dark, so...on the top of a blank page in my journal I wrote the following words: "How can I make money writing and organizing?" and trusted the universe would reveal the answer.

Several months later, I was at Loral Langemeier's Cash Machine Workshop. I didn't really know who Loral was, but a friend offered tickets and it sounded like it would be fun. And, it was! I noticed though that for some attendees, the Internet marketing strategies Loral mentioned were new and sometimes difficult to follow. On the other hand, I also met experts each of whom carried a little piece of the jigsaw puzzle all of the business owners attending needed to put together if they wanted to succeed. I asked them if they were willing to partner up and fill the gap. That is how Googlicious was born—at the Cash Machine Workshop in New Jersey! It has been truly amazing how my business has continued to grow and evolve. The fact that you are reading this book right now is just one of the many examples that creation starts in your mind.

> Whatever the mind can
> conceive and believe,
> You can achieve.
> *— Napoleon Hill*

Do you have the mindset for success?

The purpose of *Googlicious* is to help you live a rich life. A rich life is much more than having money. A rich life is about living your values, loving what you do, spending time with your family and friends, finding joy, happiness, and fulfillment in every day. It is about doing what is important to you while taking care of your body and soul. A rich life means living your true self. Do you believe this is possible? Whatever you want to achieve starts with developing the right mindset.

When you read the Internet marketing secrets in this book, know applying what we teach is doable. Don't tell yourself it is too complicated or too much work, because you might prevent yourself from getting the results you want. Often, we are better at finding excuses why something can't be done than finding the one reason that will drive and motivate us to take action despite the challenges we face. This is why it is so important to have a clear vision and stay focused on it. Your vision is the "why" that will give you the persistence needed to succeed.

Be clear on your outcome

There is a reason you picked up this book. You may feel you need to improve your online presence, get active on Facebook or improve your online networking skills. Maybe you have already started building your database, but don't know what to do next. Be specific in what you want and why you want it. A Facebook Fan page in itself isn't really a goal. What do you expect to achieve? What would you like it to do for you? More money? More clients? Or do you want to have more free time? Be clear on your purpose — like Stephen Covey says, "Start with the end in mind."

When somebody starts a business, it is always recommended to write a business plan. Even though there is great value in doing this, most business owners who don't need a loan and are not looking for investors unfortunately feel it's not necessary to write a business plan. Just like a business plan is a road map on your journey as an entrepreneur, writing your online marketing strategy will help you organize your thoughts, think about the different aspects involved, and gain clarity on your goals and how to achieve them.

Before you continue reading, grab a pen and paper or open a notepad on your computer or your phone. Take thirty minutes to write what you'd like to get out of this book. Set the intention of the results you will create for your business. As you read *Googlicious*, take notes. After each chapter you read, write down the action steps needed. Make those action steps real by scheduling them in your calendar or hiring somebody to take action for you. When you complete this book, you will have the information you need. Implementing what you have learned will allow you to achieve your online goals. You probably know the importance of writing your goals on paper, yet it is easy to skip that step. If you don't yet have your vision and purpose in writing, I highly recommend you take the time to do so.

In his book *Think and Grow Rich* Napoleon Hill recommends having a written statement of what you intend to achieve and seeing yourself already having accomplished it. This is a success principle many of the wealthiest people use. There is so much power in the written word — don't underestimate it.

Share your passion

What is your passion? Do you have a message you want to share with the world? Is there a subject about which you are knowledge-able and enjoy explaining to others? Or do you have a life story that can empower and inspire other people? You may not even be aware the information you have is of great value to others. For you, it may come so natural you take it for granted. Yet, if you would take the information out of your head and write a book, people would love to read it. From your expertise or experience you can write a book and create other information products to reach new markets all over the world. *Googlicious* will show you how, whether it is with your existing business or if you want to create another stream of income from your passion.

> I think there is something, more important than believing: Action!
> The world is full of dreamers, there aren't enough who will move ahead and begin to take concrete steps to actualize their vision.
> — *W. Clement Stone*

You can be an author!

A great way to share your passion is by writing a book. Think about it—your books can reach far away countries you didn't even know existed and touch somebody's life. Written words, from papyrus scrolls to books as we know them now, have been very important in preserving information, events and life experiences. Words that otherwise would have been lost. One person may have spent his whole lifetime researching and studying a topic and we can gather all that knowledge by reading the book he or she wrote. Napoleon Hill is one of those people who have become a legend, because his message and knowledge has impacted and continues to transform the lives of many people. Even though he can no longer share his philosophy with us, his voice can still be heard by those who read his book *Think and Grow Rich.* We can't talk with Andrew Carnegie, Henry Ford, Thomas Edison and the other successful and wealthy people whose lives he studied. We may know their modern-day successors like Richard Branson, Steve Jobs, and Oprah Winfrey; but for most of us, it is hard if not impossible to contact them and do the type of research Napoleon Hill did for more than 20 years. We can take the short cut by reading and applying the success principles from *Think and Grow Rich.* Or think about how Jesus' words recorded in the Scriptures have improved the lives of countless people who actually applied his teachings. Regardless of whether you are a Christian or not, his life lessons are of tremendous value to those who want to live a happy life.

You could start by writing an e-book. Once you are finished writing it's easy to make it a PDF file. If your e-book really solves a problem that needs an instant solution, you could make money selling your e-book with very good market research and a compelling sales page. However, in general, the perceived value of a PDF e-book is not very high. It is often better to give it away as a free gift. This can be used to generate leads when you have an opt-in box on your website. (Kathy Alice Brown will explain more in the next chapter.)

Printed books, on the other hand, have something magical (even in an e-book version on Amazon). Your book can make a difference in the lives of others. It allows you to reach many more people than you could personally talk to. Plus, the advantage for you as a business owner is, once you are an author, you can establish yourself as the expert in your field. A published book gives you credibility that sets you apart from your competition. A book is a great marketing tool you can use to create a dynamic synergy between your online and offline marketing strategy. (Make sure you read Jacqueline McCarthy's chapter about this synergy.)

Writing your book

More than 400 books are published each day. Many of them end up in a garage collecting dust. Of course, you don't want that to happen to *your* books. The key factor to making your book successful is having a game plan. *New York Times* best-sellers don't just happen — they are created!

♦ **Know the purpose**
    The first step is to ask yourself, "What do I want to achieve with my book?" There are many different reasons why somebody wants to become an author. Again, start with the end in mind. Do you want to write your life's most precious moments and special memories to leave as a legacy for your family? Do you want to write a book to grow your business? Do you want to create an extra stream of income writing about your passion? Or do you have a message you want to share with the world? Your outcome will determine what path to follow as you create the game plan for your book.

◆ **Do the research**
  Find out how much information is available on your topic.
  You might see tens of different titles on happy relationships,
  but what "fresh" angle can you give or what additional
  insights can you share? In other words, how can you stand
  out from your competitors? Who exactly will buy your
  book? Is there room for possible future books or to write
  a series of books? Your research can also provide writing
  material you can use.

◆ **Make your reader your best friend**
  Your research has given you information on your competition and on your target market. You need to know who your
  potential buyers are, what they want, what their problems
  are and the solutions you can offer. As you write, keep your
  readers in mind and write specifically for them. If your book
  is about mastering your mind to become a better golfer,
  your writing style will be different than if you write a book
  entitled *Facebook for Teens*.

◆ **Create your game plan**
  Marketing is everything, but know that the money is not in
  selling books. Jay Conrad Levinson's quotation reveals how
  you can generate the cash flow you desire: "Someone once
  asked me how much I made for my first *Guerilla Marketing*
  book. The answer? Ten million dollars. The book itself only
  paid me about $35,000 in royalties, but the speaking engage-
  ments, spin-off books, newsletters, columns, boot camps,
  consulting, and wide-open doors resulted in the remaining
  $9,965,000." As his example shows, the real money comes
  from the different ways you will develop to resell the content of your book. Before you start writing, brainstorm on
  your game plan. In chapter 7, John C. Robinson explains
  exactly how you can use your existing content to create

information products, like audios, webinars, seminars and much more. Also, think about ways you will use your book as a lead generator to get more clients for your business. Your readers are already sold on working with you, because they know the value you have added to their lives.

♦ **Pull up your sleeves — the writing begins**
You have blocked this afternoon to write, you have your coffee to make it enjoyable, you have switched off your phone and asked not to be disturbed — you are ready to write! Or at least you thought so. After looking at the empty Word document for an hour or so, you decide to get another coffee. When you come back the screen is still blank and you don't have any inspiration. Now what?

Begin with your outline. Write at least ten things you want to cover in your book. Create 5-6 questions for each of the ten sections. Once you have your outline, the best way to get started is simply to start writing. Write something ... anything! No matter what it is, it will help to start the flow. Don't be critical. You can edit later. Dedicate the time you have scheduled to the creative writing process. Don't allow yourself to get distracted. In my personal experience I find it much easier to start the creation process in my mind before I sit down to write. This way you already have the ideas of what you are going to write. Another option is to record your thoughts and have them transcribed. Continue to edit when you have your manuscript completed and take advantage of feedback from others.

As with anything else in life, the more you write, the better you will get. In reality, if you are like most entrepreneurs you want to be an author, not necessarily a professional writer. If your focus is to grow your business and increase your revenue, we can help you get your book written and published without spending years writing it.

> I've never met an author who was sorry he or she
> wrote their book... They are only sorry they did not
> write it sooner.
>
> — *Sam Horn*

♦ **Your Googlicious strategy**

When the purpose is to become the expert in your industry and increase the revenue for your business, integrate your book in your overall Internet marketing strategy. The following chapters will show you how. Set up a blog, then create a Facebook Fan page and a following for your book before the manuscript is completed. This way you will already have a database of potential clients who are interested in what you offer. Do you know that you can even get speaking engagements and pre-sell your book?

> A journey of a thousand miles
> starts with a single step.
>
> — *Confucius*

We want you to succeed!

A book is the most powerful brochure in the world. It can give you free publicity and generate extra streams of income if you make it part of your marketing funnel (as Erica Lewis will show you in chapter 6). Yet for many, writing a book will take a lot of blood, sweat, tears and too much time (and of course lots of coffee ;-). If you would love to be an author and want to take the fast track, instead of losing precious time and money doing it yourself and figuring out what doesn't work, take *your* single step to accelerate your business and contact us today. THIS IS YOUR OPPORTUNITY! If you have ever thought about writing a book or want to know how to get started, claim your FREE audio (value $49) now at *www.coauthorswanted.com/bookspecial*.

We will provide you with the marketing strategies and business-building secrets successful authors use.

As you continue reading this book and start applying the Internet Marketing Secrets we'll share with you, keep in mind that success doesn't come overnight. On the outside it may sometimes look that way, but those who have traveled the path know better. You don't wake up one morning and decide to run a marathon without any training. It takes dedication, preparation, and perseverance to make it to the finish. Achieving your dreams is like winning a gold medal: you make the sacrifices — you are up early in the morning, even if you don't feel like it, and you fight your own thoughts and doubts when reality seems to prove you are never going to make it. When you win, nobody sees beyond that moment of glory — the many years of hard work, the many nights you prayed in desperation, the many battles you lost to win this war. What Rocky Balboa said in the movie *Rocky* is so true: "Everybody gets hit in life. It's not about how many times you get hit. It's about how many times you get up after you've been hit."

You need people around you who believe in you and want you to succeed. When you are stuck, please feel free to contact me or any of the other authors at *www.getgooglicious.com*. Together we can make a difference…. and convert a downturn into an upswing!

> Always remember, you are here to love, laugh,
> heal the world and fly beyond your wildest dreams…
>
> — *Shamayah Sarrucco*

About the author

Shamayah Sarrucco helps entrepreneurs become authors, enabling them to become the expert in their field, increase their credibility, distinguish themselves from their competitors, and create extra streams of income. She is an author and an inspirational speaker motivating entrepreneurs to live by design, not by default. As a trainer and coach, she has a gift for bringing the best out of you and supporting you in achieving the results you desire. Shamayah is the founder and CEO of Live by Design LLC. You can be an author! Claim your free audio at:

www.coauthorswanted.com/bookspecial

Creating a website that gets results

Kathy Alice Brown

Your first step on this journey is to create an online presence for your business. However, you don't want to have just any website; you want a website that will give you the results you want. Kathy Alice Brown told me how many business owners pay thousands of dollars to have a beautiful and professionally designed website, and then sit back and wait for the flood of traffic and sales ... which never comes. Most entrepreneurs' websites have 3-5 pages that describe their business, list their services or products, provide an "About Us" page, and often include a small "Contact Us" link at the bottom in the footer. Is that what your website looks like? Is it really designed to get results? If you are one of the many business owners who think you are done once your website is launched, get ready to learn from the experts.

— Shamayah

> You can judge your age by the amount of pain you feel when you come in contact with a new idea.
> *-Pearl S. Buck*

Let's step back and talk about what a website is supposed to do for your business. Most people think of websites as an online version of their business card or flyer. While a serious businessperson must have an online presence today, it can be so much more than just a brochure. Your website should be an integrated part of your marketing and sales strategy.

What does your ideal client really want?

Every business has an ideal client, the one that loves what you have to offer and keeps coming back for more. Who is the ideal client for your business? What is he or she looking for?

A couple of years ago I was at a technology trade show. A man approached me at the booth and started telling me about his website, which provided news and assistance for the military and their families. "How can I make my website better?" he asked me.

I knew he was looking for a technology recommendation, but I asked him, "What does your audience want? Have you asked them?" You see, I have never served in the military nor been in a military family. I am not his ideal client. Oh sure, I could have told him his website needed certain features or a different design, but it would have only been my opinion — an opinion which may be completely wrong for the customer his site is really for.

I've seen business owners get very focused on a particular feature or look for their website. *"I want my website to have an animated dog."* Seriously! It is okay to have your preferences — after all it is your website — but always keep in mind your website primarily has to be about providing the answer or solution to your visitor's need. I cannot emphasize this enough. Your ideal client should experience a *EUREKA!* moment when he finds your site: *"Finally, the answer I was looking for!"* Once this happens, your customer's next step needs to be very easy and clear, whether it is clicking on the "Buy" button or identifying himself as a lead for you to contact.

Putting yourself in your ideal client's shoes can create a paradigm shift for your marketing which has far reaching benefits beyond your website. It really IS all about your client and what they want, rather than the list of services and products your company provides. Offline, you can listen to your existing customers to figure out what needs they have. Online, you can find a similar answer by researching what they are searching on. In the next chapter, John Limbocker will explain more about keyword research. You can also go to Yahoo answers (*http:// answers.yahoo.com/*), attend online forums to find your ideal client, or do a survey. All of these will give you a wealth of insight on how to position your business for your potential clients, both offline and online.

What is your call to action?

If you already have a website, take another look at it and decide how you can improve it. Then ask yourself the following questions: "Do I promise a solution for the problem my customer has?" "Do I tell them what the next step is to get that fix or answer?" Once you put yourself in your prospective buyer's or client's shoes, you will realize these are the very same questions they will ask when looking at your website. You can perform this exercise even if you don't have a website yet: just go to one of your competitor's websites and ask yourself the same questions.

Now that you know the kinds of questions your customers will ask when they visit your website, it is time to introduce the concept of the "**Call to Action.**" Ultimately, you want visitors to your website to quickly and easily determine whether you have the answer for their problem; and then you have to *clearly* identify what the next step is they must take to get that answer and solve their problem. This "next step" is a behavior you can control through the "Call to Action."

Often we see websites that offer a solution, but don't show

what the next step should be. This next step, or call to action, needs to be the most eye-catching feature on your website. For example, make an irresistible offer to get your visitor to take action and engage with your business instead of leaving, never to come back. Erica Lewis' marketing funnel in chapter 6 will help you understand the marketing strategy behind your call to action. Whatever your call to action is, it has to be clear and unambiguous. Your call to action could be:

- Download my free report! (In exchange for their email address)

- Request a free consultation

- Call this phone number to make an appointment before prices go up

- Buy this product (single product) while supplies last

- Shop from our catalog of products where everything is 25% off!

- Post a comment and start a conversation

- Connect with me on Twitter and Facebook

What type of website(s) do you need?

So far we have focused on a common type of website that is called a brochure website. Typically this site is static (i.e., it doesn't change very much) and is designed to provide information about your business. However this type of website is not easily found through Internet search engines, so you will have to promote it so customers can find you.

There are other types of websites you may want to build instead of (or in addition to) the brochure website. They can help generate leads or build your credibility as an expert. Many websites are a mixture of different types, customized to suit the company's needs. Let's take a look at some of these website types and how they might fit into your online marketing strategy.

Landing pages

A landing page is a single page that is focused on one topic or product. Good landing pages give the user one clear call to action and maintain the customer's focus by providing no links to other pages. There are two types of landing pages:

- **Sales pages (or sales letter)** — the purpose of this page is to sell a product. It has sales copy that promotes one product with a prominently displayed "Buy" button on the page.

- **Squeeze page** — the purpose of this page is to generate leads. This type of landing page is set up to collect names and email addresses in exchange for something of value (for example a free report).

Landing pages make "offers" to visitors. For example: I'm offering you a download of my webinar if you will give me your email address. Or: I'm offering you a discounted price on my product if you buy before Friday. A sales page should provide enough information for the visitor to make the buying decision. The offer on the squeeze page has to be compelling enough for the visitor to give you her or his email address. An exciting trend with landing pages is the use of video — Nohra Leff will tell you more about this in chapter 5. Regardless of whether you use audio, video or just text, your landing pages need to convey urgency and the need to act soon.

Landing pages are frequently used in combination with PPC (pay per click) advertising or email marketing campaigns. One of the common mistakes new marketers make is launching a campaign that does not go to a targeted landing page. Your landing page needs to match up with what is in your PPC ad copy or in the email blast. Imagine if you advertise left handed golf clubs and then sent your visitor to your home page, which has a broad overview of golfing products. Wouldn't it be better to send the visitor directly to the left-handed golf clubs product page?

Your campaign may also be centered around a specific event, such as a webinar. In this case your landing page would be a squeeze page telling them about the up and coming event and inviting them to join the "interest" list. This is a good example of gathering leads for your sales process follow-up.

Landing pages are measured by how well they convert traffic (visitors to the page) to a sale or lead. You want to test which sales copy and headline converts better. Learn about A/B testing, where you send traffic to two different versions of your landing page and track which page performs best. Don't assume you can predict your visitor's behavior. My crystal ball has failed me many times: in each case, the headline that converted the best was the one I didn't like.

> **Hint:** *setting up an account with Google Analytics will help you generate detailed statistics about the visitors to your website.*

Squeeze pages and opt-in boxes

The fields used to capture a visitor's name and email address are collectively called an opt-in box. You can place an opt-in box anywhere on your site, not just on a squeeze page. For example, many websites have opt-in boxes on their home page. You want to offer your prospects a free gift for giving you their email address.

Once you acquire the email address, you need to begin communicating with your prospects! You can use an auto responder or ESP (email service provider) to set up your email marketing campaign. Automating your lead follow-up is a powerful way to increase your sales. There are a number of excellent ESP's on the market. For a monthly fee they store your contact list, send the emails for you, and generate the opt-in box code, which your web designer can place on your website. An ESP will also keep you out of spammer trouble and in compliance with the CAN-SPAM Act of 2003 by automatically placing an unsubscribe link in your emails. When you set up your list for the first time, remember to test the opt-in process and review the emails first before trying it out on your "real" prospects and clients.

Make sure you get your leads' permission to send them email messages. You can do this in a couple ways: when someone "opts in" to your list (or when you add them manually), you send a confirmation email first with a link they have to click on to confirm they really want to join your list. This is called "double opt-in." That client you met at last week's business event may need a reminder of who you are. An invitation to join your list is a graceful yet strategic way to keep you in the forefront of their mind.

The money is in the email list! If you have a list of people who read your emails, you are building a relationship with them. As they are getting to know you better and trust you, they will be more likely to take action on your recommendations, whether you offer your own products or someone else's. Treat the people on your list with respect, continue to give them value, and you will be rewarded many times over.

Selling your products online — eCommerce sites

The best example of an eCommerce site is one that everyone knows, Amazon.com. If you want to sell your products online, spend some time on Amazon.com and pay close attention to how it works. It's a great model of eCommerce done right. The "**keep it simple" principle**, while true with any website, is especially important when you are selling products online. If the buying process is too complicated your sales will suffer.

There are two parts to an eCommerce site: (1) the catalog of products you are selling; and (2) the shopping cart. As with ESP's, you can rent shopping cart software and integrate it with your website. You will have to do some research to decide if you need a merchant account. Merchant accounts can take a week or more to get approved and have specific requirements. PayPal can be an easy alternative for lower sales volumes. If you are selling digital products, you could also use Clickbank.

What is a blog and how is it different from a website?

A blog, which is short for "Web Log," is a website. Blogs are obviously different from static websites. However the line between the two is blurring. One reason for this is because blogging software today is very flexible, allowing customization, and page creation as well as posts. For example, the dynamic nature of blogging software makes it a lot easier to add pages to a website. You don't have to know HTML, FTP, or other technical skills to publish to a blog.

The intent of a blog is to have a conversation with your audience. The blogger writes a post and visitors can comment on the post, which creates the conversation. The key concept here is **dynamic**. Search engines, such as Google, love the ever-changing content on blogs and this helps the business to be found. Having an up to date blog can establish you as an expert and greatly enhance your credibility. You want to be part of the online conversation in your area of expertise. Use blog posts, tweets (Twitter), and Facebook to get your voice out there. One of my clients added a blog to her website. I coached her on what keywords to use in her blog posts and now she gets over 1,000 visitors to her site a month. Of course, her blog is just one part of her online marketing strategy, which also includes Twitter, LinkedIn, and Facebook.

There are many free blogging services such as blogger.com and wordpress.com. Wordpress also offers software that creates a blog that you have complete control over. If you plan to blog, having your own blog is ideal.

Your blog must have a RSS feed. RSS, which is an acronym for Real Simple Syndication, is a way to publish your blog posts or web pages to other websites. RSS allows users to see what has been published on each of their favorite blogs without actually going to those sites. Try it out on Yahoo or bloglines.com to see how it works.

Conversely you can also use RSS feeds from other sites (such as news sites) on your own website. This can help your website appear more up to date with a section that is constantly changing and new. Just keep in mind that other people's content should not comprise the majority of your website.

Content sites

A content site is a website that is full of useful articles about a topic. Search engines **love** content, which is why these sites often rank better. Content sites work well with affiliate Internet marketing, but are also great for promoting your business services or products. Like a blog, which can be thought of as a special type of content site, the content website will establish your credibility as an expert.

Getting started—domains and hosting

To get started with building your own website, you will need a domain name and a hosting account. A domain name is similar to the address of a house. When you type in a website name (such as *http://www.yoursuccessfulwebsite.com*), that name is translated to a special set of numbers that tells the Internet where to find the actual website. A hosting account allows you to rent space on a server to store your website files that the domain maps to. Domain registration and setting up a hosting account are actually two different tasks — you can use separate providers for each, but if you are just getting started, use one for both.

When people start thinking about creating their website, the first thing they do is register a domain name. Your domain name is an important choice, so give it some thought before you register the name. Key questions to ask include:

- Is it easy to remember? Stay away from words no one knows how to spell.

- Does it have words that people will search on? Domains with popular keywords will help your website get found.

- Is there a call to action? Action oriented domain names that suggest a solution to a problem are catchy and memorable.

Today you have a lot of choices for domains and hosting. Many providers offer unlimited domains and space for a low price. If you are not sure about which company to pick, here is what I recommend: pick up the phone and call the ones you are considering. You want to make sure you are comfortable with their customer service team in case you run into any problems.

Conclusion

Your website is the online representation of your business. Since it is often where prospects receive their first impression of your products and services, make sure your website is welcoming and engaging. Whether you use your website for leads or online sales, it is not enough for it to just be pleasing to the eye — your website needs to guide your visitors to take action.

In this chapter, I've covered different types of websites and their uses. But I've just scratched the surface of what I would love to share with you. Get a jump on making your website successful and download my free report "*5 ways to get your website Googli-cious*" at *http://www.yoursuccessfulwebsite.com.*

For more information on the best tools and products to get you started, please visit *www.yoursuccesfulwebsite.com/resources*

The content of this chapter was current when the book was writ-ten. As technology continues to develop, you can find revised and additional information on Creating Websites for Results *at:* **www.yoursuccessfulwebsite.com/googlicious**

About the author

Kathy Alice Brown is an Internet business and SEO consultant and has been in the technology industry for 20 years. She builds optimized websites that get found and attract clicks.

Visit **www.yoursuccessfulwebsite.com** *for her free report "5 Tips to Make Your Website Googlicious."*

 **Tip from Shamayah!**

It will cost you money if your website is down. Start monitoring your website for free with Uptrends. There is no installation or software required, and it's set up within five minutes. Sign up for a FREE 4-week trial at www.coauthorswanted.com/ uptrends. If your website, server, or transaction experiences a failure, you will receive an alert via SMS, email, RSS, or IM. You will also receive detailed online reports about uptime, downtime, load time, and errors.

 # The best search engine secrets

John Limbocker

So, here you are—all excited about your new website! You have made the improvements. You have a clear call to action and are ready to start building your list. A week goes by and only a few people join your email list. Disappointed, you log in to your Google Analytics account only to find you hardly had any visitors. It is almost like having this fabulous store, but nobody comes in the door, because they can't find you. Now what? Fortunately, John Limbocker can answer that question for you. He is the founder of the SEO Dominator's Club and has over 13 years experience in helping companies optimize their websites to dramatically increase profits. I will let him tell you his best search engine secrets —

— Shamayah

> Many of life's failures are people who did not realize how close they were to success when they gave up.
> — *Thomas Edison*

Search Engine Optimization has many meanings and covers a broad range of tasks and techniques. Most people refer to it as SEO. In plain English, it simply means the process of getting your web pages listed at the top of the search engines like Google or Yahoo. Online success comes when prospective customers can find you when they search using specific terms called keywords in a search engine. If you want to succeed with SEO, you need to target the specific keywords that your prospective customers are using when they are searching. The keyword list is the backbone of any good SEO campaign. Targeting the right keyword list can make you or break you.

A typical search scenario goes something like this: Let's assume you're selling a product that reduces heartburn called "Product X." Your company and brand are called "Company X." and your ideal prospect's name is "Bob." Bob sits in front of his computer to find a solution to his problem. Bob is new to this, so he has never heard of "Product X" or "Company X." If you are only listed in the search engines using your Company, Brand, and Product names (like most websites are) you are going to miss out. Bob will never find you!

Bob starts by going to Google or his favorite search engine and enters keywords to find a solution to his problem. When he starts he is in research mode so his keywords are typically very generic. He might search for something like "heartburn." This search will bring back millions of results that are all over the place and mostly unrelated to solving his problem. He does, however, learn from this search that heartburn is also called *acid reflux* and *GERD*.

Next, Bob starts getting more specific with his search terms with searches like "Heartburn Relieve Home Remedies" or "Over The Counter Acid Reflux Pill." These are called long-tail keywords, and this is where the magic happens. When your prospects go from generic searches to long-tail searches, they are getting closer to a buying decision. They are moving from "research mode" to "purchase mode" and this is when you want Bob to find you.

To be successful selling online you need to capitalize on the traffic of these long-tail searches. The more specific the search term, the more likely they are to be buyers rather than researchers. Another factor is to use keywords that get a decent number of searches for your market situation. If your product has a higher dollar profit margin, you can focus on terms with less traffic more successfully. Think of it this way: if you make a month's income from one sale, like in real estate, then you don't necessarily need a lot of traffic. You just need the right traffic. On the other hand, if you are selling products with a ten-dollar profit, you need a much higher number of prospects to make a living, so you need to target higher volume search terms.

I will soon reveal how to find the high volume long-tail keyword phrases that your prospects are typing in and how to get your website in front of them at that crucial moment when they shift into buying mode. This is the heart and soul of SEO.

SEO is often portrayed as an ever-changing mystery that's nearly impossible for the average website owner to take advantage of because of its complexity. This couldn't be further from the truth. I will demystify SEO for you in three simple and easy to understand steps. Then I will reveal how I automate nearly the entire process, which is the secret to accelerating your success. There is no magic bullet or easy button out there. There is going to be some work on your part, but it's not complicated or too difficult.

Pay close attention now as I reveal the process I have developed to drive high quality targeted traffic to my commercial client's websites. This traffic has resulted in over one hundred million dollars in increased online sales over the past decade. I guess you could say I am fairly sure the process works at this point!

My simple process starts with choosing keywords. Then you create content based on those keywords. Next, you get outside sites to link to your site using your keywords as text links. Finally, we automate the process. I will explain each of the three steps and then come back around and show you how to simplify your life using low cost tools and services to automate these simple, yet tedious, chores.

Step #1 choosing keywords

Use Google's online keyword tool to do competitive research (*http://www.google.com/sktool*). You need a Google Adwords account to take full advantage of this tool's features. Sign up for a free account if you don't have one yet. Once open, this tool allows you to either enter keywords or a website address. I recommend entering your competitors' website addresses. If you don't know your competitors' sites, simply go to Google and run a search for your main keyword. Focus on the sites selling similar items to yours. Skip any that are not true competitors.

After entering your competitors' web address into the Google SK Tool, click the "Find Keywords" button and it will give you the top 100 related keywords. It will also give you other data related to the keywords, like number of searches per month, competition, and bid prices. We are only interested in the keywords and volume of traffic. Don't pay attention to the competition and bid prices, because they only relate to Google's PPC (pay per click) program.

Click the check boxes next to the keywords that relate to your market and have a decent number of searches. Click "Save to Draft" and move to your next web address. Repeat the process on as many competitors' sites as you like. Once complete you can export the results of your draft. Now you have a csv text file of all your competitors' related keywords and search volumes.

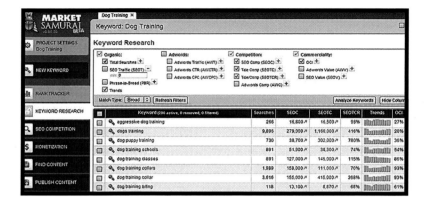

Most people stop here and use this as their keyword list, but I go a step further. I use a program called Market Samurai, which is a powerful keyword research tool. It not only gives me the long-tail versions of the keywords, but it also includes much more valuable data like organic search competition and commercial intent. Organic search competition tells us if we should even try for a certain keyword or if it is too tough to get to the top. Commercial intent gives a percentage value estimating the intent of the searcher to purchase verses research. This is extremely valuable when picking the most effective keywords to target. Market Samurai lets you cherry pick the gold from your keyword list. Take your top 10 most lucrative keyword phrases and make a list of the most effective related keywords for each of them. Use these 10 lists to create the content for 10 new SEO pages as outlined below.

Step #2 content creation

Once your keywords are defined, you need to start creating content around those keywords. Developing quality content based on your keyword list will ensure you are targeting your visitors' desires. This creates a positive user experience and enhances their comfort level, which increases your odds of them purchasing your products or services. This is why it's so important to target your keywords.

There are many types of content including text, audio, and video. Some are more effective than others for certain markets. For instance, people on the go prefer audio podcasts so they can download them on their iPod and listen while they are driving or working out. They thus turn dead time into productive time. Most audiences, especially the lazy ones (myself included), love video! Every type of content still requires at least some supporting text, so text content is always going to be the most important, even if it is minimal.

Text is used in SEO for both your on-site content and your off-site content. On-site content refers to the pages of your website. I recommend creating a page on your site for every keyword or group of closely related keywords. Use related keywords throughout the text of this page, and make the text interesting and specific to the main keyword or group of keywords. The more pages you have, the more opportunities you have for Bob to find you when he's searching for your product or services. Think of your website's pages like real estate. If you only have one property then you can only collect rent from one person. If you have ten properties, you just increased your earning potential tenfold, and so on.

Many so-called "experts" will tell you your keyword density is the key to SEO. This just isn't the case anymore. Just use your keywords naturally. Make sure you use them as much as possible without overdoing it. If they read the way you would speak, then you are probably in good shape. Some people needlessly repeat the same keywords over and over, which doesn't help; it just looks spammy and turns your visitors off.

The biggest on-page SEO factor is the use of the main keyword in your title tag. Other meta tags, like keyword and description meta tags, used to be major factors, but not anymore. As the search engines' scoring systems (algorithms) evolved, these tags lost value because they were over used. I do, however, still use them just because it is proper form and they'll probably carry more value in the future once the trendy SEO'ers lose interest in them. Focus on creating as many pages as possible with text content based on your keywords. Use your main keyword as the title of the page you are creating, because it carries the most SEO value for a particular web page.

Off-site text content is used for articles, press releases, blog posts, forums, and so on. This text should follow the same rules. Use the keyword or group of keywords, and use the main keyword in the title. The purposes for off-site content are multifold. The first is to spread your content and gain more "real estate" to drive more traffic to your site. Second is to control outside web pages and send links back to your site. You will learn the importance of these as I cover linking strategies.

Multimedia content, like audio podcasts and videos, has a very special place in SEO. Search engines don't understand the content of the audio or video files, but they do understand the titles and the descriptive text of the pages they are on. There are hundreds of Web 2.0 sites like YouTube and Facebook, where you can submit your multimedia content and links. This adds up to more "real estate" for your keywords.

You might be thinking, *"Why do I need more 'real estate' for the same keywords?"* How does removing your competition sound? Imagine owning all the hotels on a particular block. Anyone needing a room on that street would be coming to you. Convert that scenario into search engine terms and you have the following results: Bob runs a search for one of your keywords. Up comes your website, then an article site with your article on it, a video site with your video on it, a press release site with your press release on it, a blog with your post on it, a podcast of your audio, and they all point Bob back to you as the authority on the subject. Whom do you think Bob is going to buy from?

Using multiple forms of content can push your competitors

right off of the first page of search results. I call taking multiple slots like this SED, which is a term I coined for Search Engine Domination, which is my specialty!

Step #3 linking

Linking has become the single most important factor in SEO. Search engines have turned the web into a popularity contest. SEO used to be about having the best most unique and regularly updated content. Now it is about whose content is the most popular. The popularity is judged by incoming links. Each link is a vote cast in your favor. But not all votes carry equal weight. More popular sites send you a lot more "link juice," as we call it, than less popular sites. Your goal is to get as many different sites linking to your content pages as possible. Text links are best and the way the links are created is very important. The text in the link should be your keywords for the page you are linking to. This is called the "anchor text" in the link. If your page is about "Heartburn Relief Home Remedies," then you want the text linking to the page to be "Heartburn Relief Home Remedies."

SEO anchor text linking simply means using your keywords as the text in the clickable link. When search engines find links on other sites, they spider, or visit, the linked page and cast a vote for its popularity. This is known as an incoming link or a back link. If the engine finds content that is related to the anchor text, it awards additional merit to that page. Ultimately, the page with the most popularity and merit will be awarded the top spot on the search engine results.

It's a major hassle to get other webmasters to give you these optimized links. This is where all of your off-page content comes in handy. Use the many Web 2.0 sites out there to publish your SEO content. Web 2.0 sites allow you to create free accounts and load your content up to them. This gives you additional pages on these outside websites that you have control over to send links back to your site. There are thousands of these Web 2.0 sites out there. They include social media sites, video hosting sites, article directories, press release sites, podcast directories, website directories, forums, book marking sites, and millions of blogs with open comment sections, just to name a few.

You can have all the links you want using these Web 2.0 sites. They're free for the taking. Most website owners don't have a clue about this, which puts you ahead of 90% of them. I am about to hand you another 9% by giving you my resource list and showing you how to automate most of the SEO process. At that point you will lead 99% of the pack!

The secret: automation

Figuring out what to do is only half the battle. You still have to figure out how to get it done in the time you have available. The biggest key to your SEO success will be in automating most of the processes, so you can focus on your core business. Most SEO tasks can be outsourced or automated. I recommend doing your own keyword research and on-site content if at all possible. These are too crucial to put in someone else's hands. You can outsource your linking and off-page content creation like articles, press releases, and blog posts. There are tools and services to help with the rest.

Many companies specialize in ghost writing articles. There are also freelance sites, like Elance.com, where you can post your projects and find good writers. Article syndication services publish your articles to hundreds of article directories. Make sure to place your anchor text links in the resource section at the end of each article.

There are great online services to help you create videos and syndicate them to all the free video hosting sites. You can use one of the free conference calling services to create your audio files. Simply record the call and download the recording for audio content. You can use this audio as the sound track for a video slide show to create video content.

Linking networks can be really good, but be careful — they can put you on dangerous ground if they're not legitimate. If you use them, make sure they are safe and secure. They need monitoring to immediately remove any site that falls out of Google's index, and they must make sure all the sites in their network are all on different class c IP blocks in good neighborhoods.

A good link network can bring you a steady stream of incoming links that appear to be very natural from the search engine's viewpoint. Just make sure you don't get all your links in one shot and then stop. This is not natural. You should also vary your anchor text in your links because it is not natural for everyone to link to you using the same anchor text. This would immediately look contrived. To be successful your linking program should be steady and appear natural.

Imagine what having the right skills and knowledge will do for your online business. Imagine using this information to get multiple listings in the Search Engines. How much more money could you make?

As my way of saying *thank you* for purchasing this book, I'm offering you my entire resource list of tools and services to automate your SEO. This resource list, coupled with the knowledge from the SEO Dominator's Club, will put you on the fast track to online success. Get the resource list here: *http://seodominators.com/resources*

I look forward to helping turn your website into a Virtual Cash Machine!

John Limbocker
SEO Strategist

P.S. If you're serious, and would like my help Cashing In on Free Search Engine Traffic, join my SEO Dominator's Club at *http://SEODominators.com*. The club offers 24/7 access to my step-by-step video tutorials. These videos cover every step of the SEO process. It's like looking over my shoulder as I do it for you. This is your complete blueprint to success. You also get direct access to me as I answer all your questions in our weekly conference calls.

About the author

John Limbocker is a Search Engine Optimization Strategist responsible for over One Hundred Million Dollars in increased online sales for his commercial clients, through natural Search Engine Traffic. He is a well-respected speaker and author on the subject of SEO and offers online training for anyone wanting to increase their online business. John also offers commercial SEO services for larger companies. To learn more, visit http://SEODominators.com

World-class writing brings in the big bucks

Shamayah Sarrucco

If there is one skill that would greatly impact your online success, what do you think it would be? Oh, well... the title of this chapter has already pretty much given it away. You can have a great website and market your business and/or products with social media networking; but using the right words is the only way get the results you seek.

Internet marketers like Mike Dillard who are attracting big bucks attribute most of their success to their copy writing skills. My mentor, Tom Antion — who has made millions of dollars online — told me one of the main skills that made him most of his money is knowing how to write copy that compels people to buy. Even when you use audio and video on your site, somebody still needs to write the script!

> Give people things that help them and make them happy. And then sell them things that help them even more and make them even happier.
>
> — Frank Kern

Let's start with the foundational principles to help you write effectively and persuasively, whether it is for your website, blog, newsletter, or social media readers. It is important you understand the key secrets to successful writing, even when you decide to hire a company to do your writing.

◆ **Stay focused on your objective**
Before you start writing, always ask yourself what your objective is. Do you want your readers to opt-in on your website or buy your product (or service)? As you write, determine the action you want them to take when they finish reading. When you are writing to give content and develop the relationship with your reader, be clear on your objective so you can subtly pitch what you are selling. For example, when I write an article on how to become an author, I can mention my coaching program a few times throughout the article without being considered too pushy. The readers who like what I offer can choose whether or not to work with me.

◆ **Speak your readers' language**
The better you understand your target market, the better you will be able to communicate in a way that builds rapport. You want to know their desired outcome and show you genuinely care for them and share their concerns. Building rapport has to do with mutual liking, trust, and allowing your readers to feel they are understood. Make them feel confident they can achieve their desired outcome. Give them tools up front to help them on their way. If they have doubts, show them how other people just like them have overcome their obstacles.

◆ **Know your competition**
Research your competition to find out how they approach your potential clients. Review their copy and learn more

about what they are doing. Position your service or product in a way that sets you apart. Emphasize what is unique about you.

♦ **Focus on the benefits**
Your readers will always ask, "What's in it for me?" (WIIFM) — so, be sure to explain how they will benefit, instead of only mentioning the features. They might read with polite interest if you describe a hair shampoo's breakthrough amino collagen complex. However, tell them they'll get beautiful, bouncy locks like Catherine Zeta-Jones in seven days, and you will get a more responsive audience!

♦ **Be original and creative**
People love it when you are original! Dare to be different and stand out from the crowd. Ask yourself, "How can I be unique and add my personal touch?" Controversy and curiosity is what catches people's attention.

A hot and spicy blog

Setting up a blog is easy and inexpensive, which makes it a great tool to connect with your target market. However, growing a blog is not as easy. Did you know within about three months, more than half of blogs are abandoned? To prevent your blog from falling into this category, you have to plan your strategy before you start and know what is involved.

Let's start with the first of the foundational principles — you need to know what your blog's objective is. Do you want to grow your database? Build your expert status? Or use it to promote your book? Some people want to add a blog to generate more traffic to their company website. A blog is a good tool to achieve this, but more traffic is not the end goal. What do you want the visitors to do? What will your call to action be?

It takes time to build a blog and a following, which is probably one of the reasons so many are abandoned within a few months. You need to cover a topic in which your target market or niche is interested. Do they have a problem you can help them solve by reading your posts? You have to be entertaining or educating. Once you know your topic and the name for your blog, write an outline of the different subjects you want to cover and create categories for each subject. (It's best not to have too many). Using the categories as book chapters makes it easy to adapt your blog contents to book format or create other products you can sell.

The more you write, the more visitors you will attract; which is why, ideally, you should post every day. If this is too much, you can either write your blogs in advance and post them daily or at least three times per week. When you know your topics, make a schedule of what you will cover, by date, and put this in your calendar. If there are any events you will be attending, you will write about them or make a short video you can post on your blog.

How do you make your blog hot and spicy? Put your personality in your writing. Have you ever noticed the difference when somebody smiles on the phone, even when you don't see the person? It comes through in their voice. It's really funny, but the same is true with your writing, so smile when you write. Your blog gives you the opportunity to become friends with your readers and you want to connect with them. So write as if you are talking to one of your best friends. Make it conversational instead of boring and official. Keep the flow open when you write by not allowing yourself to edit until you are finished writing. One blogger even said he turns off his computer screen when he is writing to prevent himself from going back until he has put down all his thoughts. When you go back to edit, take out all the fluff. Make it easy to read and to the point — use short words, sentences and paragraphs. Step in the readers' shoes and ask yourself after each paragraph, "Did I really add value with this information?" Would the post have persuaded you to take action? Is there an invitation to comment, share, buy, or opt-in to your list? Spend most of your time on the headline, the subheads and your first paragraph. This is where you need to catch attention and draw your readers to continue reading. Also, keep in mind most people won't get to the end of your blog post.

It does make a difference as you write when you have inspiration, because your readers will feel your excitement in your words. You can keep a little notebook (or use the voice recorder on your phone) to capture thoughts and ideas for your blog during the day. Sometimes you have to write when you don't feel inspired — what do you do? Some wait until they are in the mood. I say, do whatever it takes to get yourself in the mood. From experience I can tell you it can take too long before you are in the mood and you can't keep procrastinating. As Tony Robbins teaches, you can change your emotion in a heartbeat. So, when you don't feel like writing, get yourself excited and the inspiration will start to flow. Play your favorite song, dance to the music, sing about all the great things in your life, jump up and down with your hands high in the air. I know this sounds silly, but give it a try; you will be surprised.

Blogging is about engaging and getting others engaged with you. Getting comments is valuable to create conversation and search engines love it. It can be a challenge to get people to post a response. It's estimated only 1 out of 1,000 readers will post a comment. So be patient and if somebody does post a comment, thank them for their participation. Be creative — maybe you can give away a prize or create a contest to provide incentives. You can participate in the blogging sphere by commenting on other blogs. These blog readers will get to know who you are and may click on your link and subscribe to your blog.

The world constantly changes, so stay updated on the latest trends and what is happening in your niche. You can subscribe to http://www.Google.com/alerts to be informed of blog posts that are related to your keywords.

Let your readers know each time you have posted new content, so they can come back. Most importantly — keep your objective in mind and always, always, always tell your readers what you want them to do next!

How to write your sales page

Typically, a sales page is entirely focused on a single product or service to prevent visitors from getting distracted: the objective is to make a sale. The copy writing is a little different than a blog. You want the readers to take action now! You want them to click the "buy" button and make their payments. The quality of your writing will reflect directly on your bank account.

We humans are emotional beings and we make decisions based on our emotions rather than on rational thinking. It is an art to write powerful sales copy that creates emotional heat. Understanding the psychology that makes us buy will give you the building blocks to do this. People want to know what they will get when they buy from you and they want to be convinced it will help them get their desired outcome.

Write with their interests in mind when you share how buying from you will improve their lives or businesses. Make them feel your product or service is a good value. Talk directly to your reader, as if you are talking to a friend. Work on maintaining a You versus I/We ratio of 3:1 in your copy. They still might be hesitant and doubting as to whether what you say is true. How can you overcome this challenge?

It is a human tendency to look at others and see what they are doing to ensure we are making the right decision. In his book *Influence — The Psychology of Persuasion* Robert B. Cialdini Ph.D. shares his research citing how powerful social proof is. For some reason, we seem to believe if other people are doing it, it must be the right thing to do, especially when these people are "just like me." How can you use this knowledge for your sales page? Ask clients who have already used your product or services to share their experiences with you. Make these testimonials tangible and real. What specific results did they get? Use the name, city, and state — maybe even profession — in the testimonial with a picture, so potential clients know these are real people, just like them, who benefitted from real results. You can also have a video testimonial.

Be original and creative. Come up with something different. Tom Antion had great success with the campaign he did at the end of December: "We need to make room for our new inventory before the New Year. All e-books on sale!" Normally he would not sell a lot in that period — this time he did, which is really funny, because everybody understands e-books don't take up any space. Still, the campaign worked!

The fear of potential loss makes us perceive something as more valuable. When we feel the opportunity may not be available again, we are more inclined to buy right away, even though normally, we would not really be interested. How can you use this? Make a special offer for the first X number of people who buy; after those first clients the price goes up. Make a limited number of products available or give visitors a limited time to buy. This creates a sense of urgency to take action NOW! When the offer is limited it also makes it exclusive and as we all want to feel special, gives us an extra motivation to buy.

Split-test to make your sales page even better. Creating two different sales pages that are mostly the same, but have one different component, can improve your results. For example, you only change the headline on one and when you know which one performs best, you keep that one. Next, you change something else in the wording and see which one performs best. One of my Internet-savvy friends told me he would sell more memberships when the title under his picture was "Founder of ..." instead of "CEO of..."

Upsell or downsell to meet their needs. Did you ever see one of those pop-up boxes show up just when you are about to leave a website? Believe me, they work! Somebody may not be ready to buy the product you offer for $197 on your sales page, but maybe he wants to buy your e-book for $29. Or even if somebody bought your $197 product, you can offer your e-book for a special price of $14.95. This is a powerful way to increase your revenue with one single client and it will support him in getting his desired outcome, because now he has more tools. It's a win-win!

No junkie junk emails

The money is in the database. In chapter 2 we discussed the importance of having an opt-in page on your website, so you can stay in touch. If you have a blog, you also want your readers to opt-in, so you can continue to grow your list. Once you have all these emails collected how do you win their friendship and make them feel you are the expert? Nobody likes to be sold to, but we do want to buy from somebody we like and trust.

Most people are so swamped with spam that if they don't know the sender they are not likely to open the email. In fact, 23% of the emails are deleted unopened. What can you do to have the people on your list open and read your emails? Implement the following tips:

◆ Use an email address that is easy to recognize and use the same email address for all your emails. Of course, using a free email account is not the smartest thing to do, because most of the junk is coming from a hotmail, Gmail, or similar account.

- Create a subject that catches people's attention.

- Use their first name in the subject. Many sources show personalizing subject lines gets up to a 64% increase in email open rates. It's very easy to merge their name if you use, for example, 1shoppingcart.

- Give value to get potential customers in the habit of opening your emails. They need to be excited to get your emails, because they know they will learn something. Continue to educate for free. This will build trust and rapport.

- Focus primarily on providing value without pushing to sell anything. If you do send out a promotion, make an irresistible offer. Make the people in your database feel special, because they are on your email list.

About the author

Shamayah Sarrucco helps entrepreneurs become authors, enabling them to become the expert in their field, increase their credibility, distinguish themselves from their competitors, and create extra streams of income. She is an author and an inspirational speaker motivating entrepreneurs to live by design, not by default. As a trainer and coach, she has a gift for bringing the best out of you and supporting you in achieving the results you desire. Shamayah is the founder and  CEO of Live by Design LLC. Claim your free audio at www.worldclasswriting.com

 **Tip from Shamaya**

You can test an autoresponder and shopping cart system that makes you money for 30 days for free at:

www.coauthorswanted.com/shoppingcart.com

Video marketing makes you money

Nohra Leff

Your little baby boy wobbling on his feet while taking his first steps; your dog acting silly; or your grandmother's 90th birthday. These are all priceless moments. It is great to have pictures, yet nothing brings those great times back to life better than video. When you see the movement and the facial expressions, when you hear the sounds and taste the atmosphere, it's almost as if you are there. Video touches our emotions — which is the essence of successful marketing. That is why video is such a powerful tool. It can give you better results, in less time and at a lower price. And the time you save (which is my favorite benefit) can now be used in a better way in your business or personal life. In chapter 3, John Limbocker mentioned briefly how videos can drive traffic to your website; in this chapter Nohra Leff will tell you exactly how to do this —

— Shamayah

> A picture is worth a thousand words.
> — *Napoleon Bonaparte*

The online universe is immense. There are over one billion Internet users worldwide. How would you like to effectively grab your visitors' attention? How would you like to convert leads into customers and put more cash in your pocket? In this chapter, I will show you how to improve the visibility of your online presence, drive massive traffic, and convert your leads into deals.

Do you remember the time before the Internet? Yes, once upon a time there was a world where there was no television; where brushes, encyclopedias, and vacuum cleaners were sold door-to-door; where the largest companies occasionally would spring for a two-color advertisement in a magazine; and where the Internet was not even a dream. But the world changed drastically and would never be the same after the television, the personal computer, and (eventually) the Internet was invented.

Today, in addition to the one billion Internet users there are over 2.2 billion mobile phone users capable of receiving video. More than 52% of Internet content today is in video form. According to the Interactive Advertising Bureau, more than 50% of the U.S. population watches online videos. This is over 155 million people — just in the U.S.!

A business owner today can make thousands, hundreds of thousands, even millions of dollars on the Internet — sales made automatically while he relaxes on the golf course or at the pool, even while he sleeps. At first, an Internet presence meant creating a single web page to give information to the Internet surfer. There was no interaction, no online sales, no live chat, no animation, and no video. The large companies wanted to be different and started adding animation, multiple pages, and interaction to their sites. They soon discovered the costs to do this were high. However, thanks to advancements in technology, it is now possible for you to utilize online video to reach a huge audience for a minimal investment. (For more information on how to create a website that delivers results, see also Kathy Alice Brown's content in Chapter 2.)

So, what makes video the most powerful marketing tool in the world?

- Video creates trust and credibility—Video builds rapport with your potential customers. They get a feel for who you are. As they start connecting with you on this personal level, trust grows.

- Video makes your viewers look at you as an authority—You shine through.

- Video marketing produces results — Online video can bring in new business. It can get the ball rolling on that elusive buzz marketing campaign.

- Video creates desire for your product or service—You can use the visual experience to build excitement for the product or service being sold.

- Video converts traffic into leads, and leads into customers—64% of the respondents in a recent study commissioned by Google and AOL have taken some demonstrable action after seeing an online video. For example, 44% went to the advertiser's website, 33% searched for a product or service, 22% visited an actual off-line store, and 21% discussed the advertised product with friends or family.

- Video marketing has a potential worldwide audience of billions—The number of people with Internet access is growing exponentially. Just think about the audience being introduced to the worldwide web in China. Imagine the growth resulting from the spread of computer technology to other developing countries.

- Video marketing is cheaper, faster, and therefore better than conventional marketing—Video marketing is no longer exclusively for the large companies who have money to spend. Regardless of whether you are a small business owner or just starting your business, you, too, can add the magic of online video to your website, particularly your squeeze page or landing page.

- ◆ Video marketing never stops working — A video properly launched on the Internet lives on and on. Proper distribution of your video can gain you almost instant attention by the major search engines. It can continue bringing leads long after you have forgotten you even made the video.

When you put a video on the Internet, you are once again that door-to-door brush salesman, but instead of walking for miles, knocking on doors, putting up with yapping dogs, or having doors slammed in your face; potential customers are now inviting you into their homes. You make your pitch once, and your effort is repeated over and over again electronically. It's as if you sent an army of salesmen into the world — but it is just you on your one short video. Now, imagine the growth of your business if you put a second video out there, or 10 more, or 100 videos!

According to COM Score, Americans watch over nine billion online videos monthly. In the Google/AOL study, 75% of respondents reported watching more video online than they did a year ago, and over half expect to watch more online video in the next year. Moreover, 78% feel online video ads provide as much or more opportunity to learn about a product or service than television, and 63% said they prefer video site advertising if it helps keep content free. The study also found online video ads resulted in 32% of viewers describing the featured brand as innovative, 32% as creative, and 30% as fun. As technology attempts to play catch-up with consumers' appetites for edgy, informative, and relevant advertising, online video technology is poised to lead the race in delivering considerable revenue to forward-thinking companies.

Getting started

Okay, you are convinced video marketing is the way to go and you are excited to use it. How do you get started?

- WHY: Know your Purpose. What is the message you want to convey? Do you want to share information to educate your audience? Or do you want them to buy your product or service to solve their problem?

> Start with the end in mind.
> — *Stephen Covey*

- WHAT: Identify your business Category and Niche. It is important to know to whom you are talking. For example, in chapter 8, Nadia Semerdjieva explains how to find your target market and how to communicate with them effectively.

- HOW: Plan the details and create the content. What should you say on your video? Well, first of all, you don't want to shoot from the hip. You need to have a script. The script should start by explaining to your viewer what you are offering, then it should move on to how it will help them, and then finish with a call to action — which explicitly identifies what you want them to do next. The call to action might be completing an opt-in form on the squeeze page they are watching, or making a phone call, or going to your website. Whatever it is, the viewer needs to be told precisely what you want him or her to do next — don't leave it to guesswork. Here are six steps you can take to create quality video content:

1. **Brainstorm to develop a good offer.** It has been shown the mere presence of video catches the prospect. Make them the right offer (something free always seems to interest the

consumer) and you turn that prospect into a lead. It is the OFFER, not necessarily the quality of your production, that converts traffic into leads.

2. **Find a good location.** No need to spend large sums on lighting. Simple, decent lighting is okay. Natural lighting from the sun is best — sit outside or sit opposite a big window. The most important factor in choosing a setting is it should result in good audio quality. The setting should be quiet with no background noise. You will discover great video has a great sound track — as clear as a radio. When appropriate, you can use your setting to make your company look bigger and more professional by showing your office, your workshop, etc. — whatever makes you look good.

3. **Practice.** Have an outline prepared and practice what you are going to say. Caution — you want your video to sound spontaneous and conversational, not scripted.

4. **Decide how to shoot the video?** You could spend tens or hundreds of thousands of dollars producing the perfect marketing piece. Then again, you can be almost as effective and much more economical by just pointing a video camcorder in your own face and recording yourself talking about your business or your product. For a longer video, consider having a friend or business partner interview you. They ask the questions and you provide the answers by talking about your business. Make sure the sound is clear and your viewers don't get motion sickness from the moving image.

5. **Ready? Take 1!** The most important thing to include is your personality. Be yourself. Phoniness comes right through the camera, but so do honesty and trustworthiness. You want to be trusted. Don't be an actor. Don't create a character. Be

yourself. Smile. If you are a nerd, let your nerdiness come through. If you are the type of person for whom everyone wants to buy a drink, let that come through. Just be yourself. Talk to the camera as if it is a real person. Look the camera in the eye, because when the video is played your customers will feel as if you are talking directly to them.

6. **Extras.** To enhance your video you might want to cut to graphics or shots of your product. You also might want to add some music from an inexpensive royalty-free music library.

> Do not wish to be anything, but who you are and try to be that perfectly.
> — *St. Francis of De Sales*

The 10 × 10 × 4 formula

Michael Koenings, co-founder of Traffic Geyser, suggests what he calls "The 10 × 10 × 4 Formula: A Magical Traffic Magnet System that Attracts Customers Like CRAZY to Any Website." He suggests you start by writing down the top ten frequently asked questions about your product or service. You also write down the top ten questions your potential buyer *could* be asking. Once those 20 questions are written, Koenings suggests you record 20 short videos answering each question. Each video should be 30 seconds to three minutes in length. In addition you create four short "mini" videos titled:

- ♦ **"To Get More, Go Here,"** which tells the viewers where to go to get all 20 videos and takes them to a Video Lead Page,

- ♦ **"Enter Your Name and Email to Get All 20 Videos,"** which appears on your video lead page and renews your connection with the viewer and explains why they should sign up,

+ **"Thank You for Signing Up,"** placed on a thank you page and telling the person who just completed your form they will receive their video as soon as they click a confirmation link being sent to their email, and

+ **"Buy My Stuff,"** which you should place on your web page and on all outgoing emails.

What do you do with your completed videos?

You will definitely want to embed video onto your squeeze pages and other locations on your websites. But you also will want to put freestanding video out there to be picked up by search engines. Letting the established video sites, such as YouTube, host your videos is a great entrée into the search engines. And the search engines are what will drive the traffic to your business.

Video marketing owes a great deal of gratitude to YouTube. YouTube is a video sharing website where users can upload, view, and share video clips. As of 10/31/09 there were 209,000,000 online videos uploaded to YouTube. This is amazing considering it was only on April 23, 2005, the first video was uploaded to YouTube. That video was entitled, "Me at the Zoo." YouTube, which has 300 million worldwide visitors a month, is the dominant online video provider in the U.S. with 100 million visitors watching more than six billion videos monthly — a market share of around 43%. It is interesting to notice the younger generation searches on YouTube rather than Google. Interestingly, in addition to YouTube there are several other video sharing sites.

Getting your video seen

When you upload your videos to hosting sites, it is crucial to have the right title and description (these should both start with the same words), file name, and tags attached. Your description should be full of keywords, and your tags should pick up words from both your title and your description. This is how the search engines will find you and send traffic to your videos. It's a good idea to also search the hosting sites for videos from people in the same business as you. Post a video response to their video. This is great for building viewers' confidence in your expertise.

Creating traffic

Let's talk a little bit about traffic — the term used for the volume of hits on your site. You need to get visitors to your website. Accomplishing this is an art. There are websites which allow you to upload your video and which then automatically distribute the video to whatever social networking/video sharing sites you choose. TubeMogul offers this service for free; others, like Traffic Geyser, do it a little better for a fee. Choosing the right title, key words, and file name are all important in getting your video picked up by search engines.

A great way to share videos with your social media networks is to tweet your video. There are a number of services you can use to tweet videos directly from your Blackberry, iPhone, or your laptop like:

- 12seconds.tv (*http://12seconds.tv*) — videos are limited to 12 seconds, but can be posted both to Facebook and Twitter;

- Yfrog.com (*http://yfrog.com*) — tweet both pictures and videos; and

- twitvid.com (*http://twitvid.com*) — where you can tweet videos

Getting more bang for your buck

Once you have made a video, transcribe it and post it as a page of text on your website. The search engines will pick up the words and direct even more traffic to your website or squeeze page. Once people get to your squeeze page or website, your goal is to get them to take the action you ask of them. The action might be giving you their email address, calling you, signing up for something, or giving you money.

Search engines

Google is the number one search engine and provides a good experience for its users. Google loves to see words on pages; Google also likes to have *video on pages*. To serve its customers, Google sends its spider programs throughout the Internet. These programs will locate your web pages, look at your content, and figure out if what is on your page matches the searcher's interest. Therefore, the more words, the more videos, and the more pages you have online; the more traffic you will attract, and the more money you will be able to put in your pocket.

Online video marketing is the key business differentiator for web companies wanting to effectively communicate their product profile and benefits within the shortest possible time. There is nothing else that comes close to the effectiveness and persuasion power of a well designed video message. This doesn't mean putting a 10-minute video tutorial on your site will automatically double your conversion rate of new registrants or instantly sell more products. There is more to effective video communication than just throwing some video content on your web pages. Every video you create is an asset. The first 30 seconds will make you or break you.

What are the trends and future of online video marketing?

Will the professional, longer videos overpower the smaller, three- to ten-minute videos? Opinions differ. Chris Tolles, CEO of the online news portal Topix, thinks video will be increasingly important. He made the following predictions concerning the future of online video:

- **Increase in scale.** Video content and activity will increase in the local online space.
- **Production key to manage.** This is in regard to cost, time and project scale, which Chris believes will be more of a priority for local campaigns than for larger-scale audiences.

- **Very short format.** Successful local video campaigns will need to be very, very short. "There's a cycle of 12 seconds (for online engagement) that's sort of interesting," says Chris. "People may want a 5-second or 10-second video of something. They don't want an hour."

- **User-generated content will dominate.** Successful local video campaigns will be based on authentic, audience-pro-duced video as opposed to professionally produced videos. "Somewhere along the line, integration of video from an audience standpoint is going to come out. It's going to be something where a video of a store or of the (customer) experience I think will be part of the process ..."

In contrast to Tolles' prediction, COM Score, a marketing research company providing marketing data and services to many of the Internet's largest businesses, already shows the average video viewer can handle over three minutes of video before getting an itchy trigger finger. Grant Crowell, the Founder of Grantas-tic Designs, an online marketing solutions firm specializing in search-optimized, user-friendly web design and multimedia content, also disagrees with Chris. "Production value also means good production quality, and one professionally produced video testimonial and review would not only be much more likely to have better influence and reach than a bunch of amateur-looking videos, but also be more visible in keyword searches and social media sites—AND provide a level of influence over the message—which businesses desperately want and need."

Either way, search traffic and engagement reports have already shown...people DO want video commentary, they DO want video reviews; they also want instructional videos, interview videos, demo videos, event videos—the whole gamut. Businesses that use video to showcase their personality and passion will be successful using video. Businesses that fail to incorporate video, or who make detached 10-15 second commercials, will be left behind wondering why no one is sharing or caring about their content.

Where to get the right help doing this whole video marketing thing

Still not sure how to get started on making your own quality video? We make it easy by producing and positioning a winning video for you. Visit our website at *http://www.videomarketing-makesyoumoney.com* and provide us with your contact information. We will get in touch with you and we will help you create a video presence that will increase your business. Are you new to video marketing, or just too busy? We will help you prepare your script, write unique content to reach your target audience, coach your performance, record your "spokes-video," and upload your video to YouTube and social networks thereby increasing your visibility to search engines such as Google.

If you are muttering to yourself that this information is outdated, pat yourself on the back...your attitude is perfect for learning about technology as the rate of technology development continues to accelerate. *Technological writing, which is accurate when put to paper, is already old news by the time of publication. That's why you should not consider your reading complete without continuing to my blog at **www.videomarketingmakesyoumoney.com** for the latest updates in video marketing.*

About the author

Nohra M. Leff is the founder of www. videomarketingmakesyoumoney.com.  *She helps small business clients establish a video presence on the Internet and use video marketing to increase their revenue. Nohra has held top leadership positions in her community. Outside of work, Nohra is happily married and a very proud mother and grandmother. She can be reached at* **www.realhopesforbusiness.com**

 **Tip from Shamayah!**

Start using video email. It is a great way to shorten the sales cycle, create instant rapport with prospects, and increase your click-through rates. Imagine what video email can do for your business. It's fun, easy, and effective! Sign up for a FREE 30-day trial at **www.coauthorswanted.com/videoemail** *and test it out for yourself.*

# Your online marketing strategy

Erica Lewis

Marketing and sales are the soul of your business. As Loral Lange-meier explains it, "Marketing is about targeting people who have a need that you can address and getting them to respond to you. It is about engaging the customer or consumers. Selling is a way of final-izing that response through a transaction. Selling is about enrolling them." You see, the marketing funnel can make a huge difference for your business once you understand it and create it the right way, because it will increase sales. Believe me, you want to know what Erica Lewis has to say —

— Shamayah

> The man who will use his skill and constructive
> imagination to see how much he can give for a dollar,
> instead of how little he can give for a dollar,
> is bound to succeed.
>
> *— Henry Ford*

To survive, every business needs customers to buy its goods and services. Many new entrepreneurs believe that if they simply create a product or service and put it online, customers will search and find them. It's not that simple. You need to take steps to identify prospective customers (generating leads) and then draw them in to actually purchase your product or service (converting leads into customers). All businesses — especially new ones — have to let people know three key things:

7. Your business exists

8. What products and services you offer

9. Why people will want to do business with you

A marketing plan allows you to identify prospective customers, what they need, how you will meet those needs one or more times, and how you will reach them. The most successful businesses are those that retain customers over a long period of time. It is often said that the hardest sale to a customer is the first one. Once they have purchased something from you, you have begun a relationship with them and they are more likely to purchase more of your products or services in the future.

If you want repeat customers who stay with you over time, structure your business using a concept called the **marketing funnel.** The marketing funnel gradually moves people from being interested in your products or services to investing more time and money in your business as they recognize and value the benefits you are providing them. Behind the marketing funnel is the intent to engender trust and build a relationship with prospective clients; and convert them into customers and possibly advocates for your product or service. The purpose of the marketing funnel is to serve your customers' needs — not to get the most money from them. Your intention must be to serve your clients and not take advantage of them. A powerful way to demonstrate this intent is to always provide enormous value and outrageous deals.

The marketing funnel involves these basic components:

♦ The business builds a database of prospective customers and markets to this list, offering products and services to solve their customers' problem(s).

♦ Many prospective customers are captured at the top of the funnel.

♦ A percentage of your prospective customers convert to actual customers when they first purchase an item, usually requiring a relatively low investment of money or time.

♦ Over time, an increasingly smaller number of them move down the funnel to purchase products and services of increasing value and requiring greater commitment of time and money.

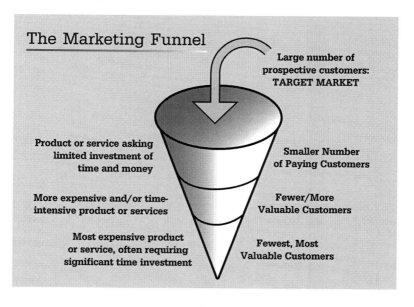

The Marketing Funnel

Large number of prospective customers: TARGET MARKET

Product or service asking limited investment of time and money

Smaller Number of Paying Customers

More expensive and/or time-intensive product or services

Fewer/More Valuable Customers

Most expensive product or service, often requiring significant time investment

Fewest, Most Valuable Customers

Identify your target market

It is both impractical and ineffective to market to every person who uses the Internet. To maximize your efforts, define your target market. Who is your target customer? What are their demographics? What do they care about and need? Narrow your target market as much as possible so you can craft appropriate offerings and crisp messages.

> Let's take one example. *Dr. Moses is a Board-certified cardiologist practicing in a large city. He often sees patients who have weakened their hearts and bodies through poor dietary choices and sedentary lifestyles. Although he often counsels his patients to eat well and exercise, he wants to work with people before they get to the stage where they need a cardiologist. He envisions a part-time practice providing preventive health tips and solutions to patients. His target market is urban residents who are at risk of developing heart problems but have not yet needed medical treatment.*
>
> Here's a second example: *Coach Jenkins has been a high school track and field coach for the last 20 years. He was instrumental in the training and development of several track and field Olympic medalists. He now wants to create a business utilizing his skills to supplement and possibly replace his income. Coach Jenkins has a clear target market: children who aspire to make it to the Olympics in track and field.*

With a more defined market, you will more easily identify ways to learn about prospective customers — a process known as **market research**. You will find single professional women by finding, learning about, and joining their most popular organizations, publications, and websites. Learn more about your target client by joining Yahoo Groups, Facebook Groups, and other forums for your target market. Through this research, you will become extremely knowledgeable about their problems and challenges.

If you know your target market well, you can build a reputation by becoming their source of effective and valued services and products. Market research is essential for two reasons: you need to know how to find and communicate with your target market. You also need to know what kind of products and services they consume. This will allow you to tailor your products and services to serve your target market well.

The top of the funnel—your potential customers

As an entrepreneur you should know how to build and maintain a database of potential customers made up of people in your target market. Your database is your profit center and an invaluable asset. Because many will not convert into customers, you will want to maximize the number of prospective clients with whom you will communicate about your product or service. The more people who might enter your funnel, the better your chances of having a good number of customers.

You build your database by attracting people to your website and enticing them to "opt in" by giving you their name and e-mail address. The most effective way to get people to opt in is by offering them something of value for FREE. You get something more valuable than money: permission to market to these potential customers *and* their contact information. Your database can be built using several different methods. You can create a new database, use prospect lists that already exist, or both. Match the communication medium to your target group.

Create a new database

+ Use the same groups, publications, and websites you consulted for market research. They will be your best lead source for prospective customers because they cater to your target market.

♦ Write your own blog, comment on other people's blogs who serve a similar market, build a Twitter following, enter discussions on Yahoo! Groups, Facebook, and LinkedIn; post informational videos on YouTube, write articles for digital and printed publications, or network at industry events.

♦ Use search engine optimization (SEO) techniques for your website and product.

♦ Advertise on the web, the radio, and television; in publications; through direct mail or post card campaigns; and by distributing flyers. Choose advertising methods that make the most sense for your target market.

♦ Create Google Adwords ads using keywords related to your product. These ads will direct prospects to your website and can be placed on sites with similar products and services.

♦ Ask for names from your friends, colleagues, neighbors, and various communities to which you belong (town, school, clubs, hobbies, etc.).

♦ Publicize your expertise and products by going on radio shows, holding seminars and webinars, and speaking in your community (e.g., the public library).

Use existing databases

♦ Joint venture with other business owners where you use their list to market your products or services in return for giving them monetary consideration, reciprocal use of your list, or some combination of the two.

Part of marketing is trial-and-error. As you gain experience using various marketing methods, you can assess, over time, which method most effectively attracts people to your site, particularly people who will purchase your product or service.

Example 1: *Dr. Moses can reach a local and a much broader target market. His strategy for getting prospective customers to the top of his marketing funnel may include getting in front of organizations, writing a blog, a monthly newsletter about preventive health methods, and articles. He can join groups on Yahoo! and Facebook, submit comments to health-related blogs, and contribute to websites that focus on cardiovascular health. As an expert, Dr. Moses can offer local and national advice on radio, TV, and Internet talk shows. In all of these venues, he can discuss his offerings and advise people to visit his website.*

To entice people to go to his website and give him their contact information, Dr. Moses can offer a free report: "Tips for Preventing a Trip to the Cardiologist." With the report, he delivers value well before asking anyone to consider spending money.

Example 2: *Coach Jenkins could offer a free one-hour information session at the local elementary and middle schools for parents who think their children have talent. This session could be videotaped and put on YouTube. He could promote it on Olympic and other track-and-field sites. To get people to give him their contact information, he could offer a free report: "What It Takes to be an Olympic Medalist in Track and Field."*

Constructing the funnel

Now it's time to plan exactly what to offer your customers, using the marketing funnel concept. People will spend money to solve problems and alleviate pain or to attract pleasure. Which of your target market's problems will you address with your product(s) and services? How will you deliver your solutions or how do you add pleasure? How do you plan to serve your customers over time? How will you deliver value and build trust and loyalty among your customers?

Before you can get a prospective customer in your funnel, you must decide:

- What products and/or services you will offer at every step of the funnel
- When you will offer these to potential and repeat customers
- Where you will offer your products and services
- How often you will make offers to your target market
- What value you will offer to make it irresistible for people to buy your products and services, and
- How often and through what media you will communicate with your customers

Converting prospective customers into paying customers

The most costly component of marketing is the "front end" or moving prospective customers into your marketing funnel through a purchase. New customers will invest only a little time and money at the top of the funnel because they lack a relationship with you and your business. At this point, the most important marketing task is to make it easy for potential clients to take the first step to becoming a customer. You will do this by offering something of ENORMOUS value to them for a very small cost.

Example 1: *One way Dr. Moses can attract his first paying clients is by offering in-depth webinars on cardiovascular health with Q&A on various topics for a small fee (say $9.95 each). If someone buys the entire webinar series, they could get a discount. Or he could offer live seminars on different preventive health subjects.*

Example 2: *Coach Jenkins could offer a reasonably priced book on how to develop highly successful athletes, based on his coaching career. Or he could run a low-cost two-hour seminar or webinar that gives a point-by-point outline of what training and development is required to become an Olympic-quality track and field competitor, with bonus tips on how to assess your child's ability.*

Moving customers through the funnel

Once customers are in your funnel, you have the opportunity to offer them more solutions to their problems. At every stage, a customer wants a good deal. Think of the first purchase as a first date. Most people aren't ready to commit to a long-term relationship with someone they've just met. Most customers also need time and repeated exposure to your business before they are ready to purchase another product or service from you.

When a customer's life improves because of your product or service, they are likely to want to continue buying from you. The rest of the marketing funnel contains products of increasing value to offer to your client base. The top of the funnel has the least expensive products, while the highest priced products or services are at the bottom of the funnel. Customers who purchase at the bottom of the funnel make a significant investment in your business, indicating great trust and loyalty.

Diverse products and services

When starting out, you may have just one product in mind. Build on that one product quickly so business doesn't depend on it alone. You want revenue from multiple items at the same time. If any one product or service stops selling, you have others to compensate. In the next chapter, John C. Robinson will provide more details on how you can create additional products.

Creating a diverse product line is not hard. Here are some simple ways to get started:

♦ Offer your expertise and information in many ways: through blogs, newsletters, periodic free reports, articles, webinars, live seminars, and one-on-one coaching.

♦ Convert your information from one format to another. Transform blog posts into a book that can be sold separately and at live events. Record live seminars and webinars, packaging them as DVDs, audio programs, and e-books.

A diverse array of products and services will not only allow you to serve your existing clients well, but they will also establish you as an expert, build your credibility, and help you attract new customers.

Example 1: *In the middle of his funnel, Dr. Moses can offer daylong seminars with in-depth information and hands-on learning to help people take control of their health. At the very bottom of the funnel, Dr. Moses could work individually with people to do a personalized assessment and create a personal health improvement plan. This would include a continuity plan that would have him monitoring his client's health through quarterly or monthly visits. Because customers would get so much of his time and effort, they would pay more.*

Example 2: *As mid-priced offerings, Coach Jenkins can create a series of audio CDs and DVDs aimed at motivating athletes and providing coaching tips. Further down in his funnel, he could offer group coaching for kids with the drive and athletic talent to potentially become world-class track and field athletes. Finally, he could offer one-on-one coaching for a high price to a few select kids with parents willing and able to make the commitment.*

Massive value through bundle packages

With a variety of products and services, you can deliver more value to your customers by creating bundles of products to offer to your customers. Bundled products deliver substantial value for a price that is far lower than if each individual item were purchased separately. For your business, bundle packages are a fast way to increase profits by bringing in more revenue than from a single sale. It's a win-win scenario.

Calls to action

At every stage of the marketing funnel, give your customer a clear and motivating call to action (*BUY NOW!*). Tell them you are offering a great deal and reward them for taking action.

A great way to spur customers into action is by creating *real limitations* (e.g., limited quantity available, first come/first serve, limits on the number someone can buy, available for a specific time only), or an air of exclusivity (limited edition, first people to get offer). Customers must take quick and decisive action to get the product or deal. Remember: to maintain trust, you must visibly honor the limit.

Bonuses are another way to inspire action, especially if they are contingent bonuses. You can offer a lower price to the first 50 buyers, give a money-off coupon to people who purchase a certain amount of products or services, or provide a free gift with purchase.

Filling out your funnel

You know your products or services are excellent and that your customer can benefit from all of them. Whenever you have your clients' attention — whether at an event or when they receive a product — immediately offer them another product or service. You are more likely to sell them something else when you have their attention.

Upselling

"Upselling" is when you offer customers a more value-laden product or service that asks for a greater commitment of time or money, or both. If the customer does not buy that, offer a product of equal or lesser value to the thing they just purchased. This is called "downselling." Other ways to support customers and bolster your relationship with them include:

+ **Continuity programs** (e.g., an online fee-based community with exclusive material)
+ **Customer loyalty programs** (e.g., buy 12, get the next free)
+ **Affiliate programs** (customers get a percentage of purchases made by anyone they refer).

Testimonials

Get customer testimonials from people who have purchased things on each level of your marketing funnel. They are a powerful way to gain credibility with prospective clients and existing customers. Expect your customers to communicate with each other and with prospective clients on social media. Because complaints travel fast, real testimonials and effective customer service are essential.

Testing your funnel

Now that you have the basis of the marketing funnel, you can build one for your business. Test your funnel at various stages of the process. Evaluate how many customers are being converted through each strategy and tactic. Assess the effectiveness of your communication program in moving customers through the funnel. One of your goals is to turn your prospective customers to loyal customers through each contact. You can have great products and services, but people won't buy if you have a weak call to action, confusing instructions, or unclear descriptions of the value of your products and services.

Your marketing funnel will evolve as your target market's needs and problems change. Stay current with your market research. Interact with your customers to assess whether your products and services are meeting their needs or if there are additional ways you can serve them. You also will grow and change, and as you do, you may want to offer different products and services over time. Service is at the heart of the marketing funnel. If you build trust and provide outrageous value with great customer service, many customers will grow loyal to your business.

For more ideas and information relevant to growing your business, visit my website at *www.ericalewis.com/welcome.*

> Marketing is not an event, but a process . . .
> It has a beginning, a middle, but never an end, for it is a process. You improve it, perfect it, change it, even pause it. But you never stop it completely.
> — *Jay Conrad Levinson*

About the author

Erica Lewis is an entrepreneur, speaker, trainer, coach, and lawyer based in New York City. She grew up in an entrepreneurial family with parents and grandparents who owned small businesses for many years. She received a Bachelor of Arts in economics from Barnard College-Columbia University and a law degree from Harvard Law School.

For articles and information on various aspects of entrepreneurship, visit **www.erica.lewis.com/welcome**

 **Tip from Shamayah!**

Can you use more help with creating your online marketing strategy? Listen to the live interview with marketing strategist Stefanie Hartman, who works with top industry players such as T. Harv Eker, Matt Bacak, Eric Lofholm, and Cynthia Kersey:

www.coauthorswanted.com/stefanie

The power of information and joint ventures

How to create and sell Information Products online

John C. Robinson

For your business to grow online, you will need to have products to sell. Where do you start? How do you create the products to fill your marketing funnel? If you offer a service where you get paid for your time, you will especially love John C. Robinson's chapter, because he will show you how you can create leverage by selling more than just your time. You can sell your knowledge! What do you know that can benefit others — your expertise, your life experience? Don't worry if you doubt whether you have knowledge that has value — just keep reading, because you will find you have more to share with the world than you thought. John will show you how to discover what it is and how to get the information out of your head and in a format you can sell —

— Shamayah

> We make a living by what we get,
> we make a life by what we give.
> — *Winston Churchill*

So, why create information products?

Well, as we learned in the former chapter about the marketing funnel:

- ◆ Initial acquisition of a marketing database of customers is a painstaking task
- ◆ Yet, the majority of your prospects will be captured at the top of your marketing funnel
- ◆ Offering something of value for FREE is one of the best strategies to get people to opt in to your list
- ◆ Creating a robust and dynamic line of products and services in your marketing funnel is often easily achieved simply by packaging information in different ways; and
- ◆ Establishing yourself as a credible expert in your market niche helps you attract new customers

The good news is that, once established, the content of your Information Products can be repurposed many times into new streams of revenue for your business. Let's explore where the content for these products can be found and how you can organize the content into cash-producing widgets for your business.

The fortune inside your head

Where does the "information" in Information Products come from? Well, it comes from what you already know! Here is a recipe to unlock the veritable fortune hidden inside your head. As you review this recipe, always remember: *you are the undiscovered hero in your business. In fact, you already have everything you need to drive your business to unlimited success.*

So, here's the recipe:

1. Tap into your **Burning Desire** and use it as a source of inspiration as you identify your **Greatest Skill Sets**

2. Determine what it is you know about these skills that can be transformed into something of **Value**

3. Create an **Information Product** around that **Value**; and

4. Integrate the **Information Product** into your business to spawn unlimited streams of revenue

To access your Burning Desire, ask yourself what you want. Don't treat this trivially — dig down deep and ask yourself what you *really* want. Now, imagine your life, as it will be when you are already in possession of everything you want. *Where will you live? What will you do with your time? Who will you interact with on a daily basis?* At this point, you are expressing your true intent or life's purpose. Indeed, this is your Burning Desire.

You will probably not have much trouble identifying your greatest skill sets. Once that task is done, however, you need to determine what it is you know about the skills you possess that can be transformed into something of value. Value is most easily recognized when someone let's you know they would like to purchase what you have. For example, consider the computer guru who is always helping his friends resolve their computer problems but never accepts their gracious offers for compensation. When should this guru stop giving away this valuable expertise for free and start charging for it? How often have you committed the same mistake? As an entrepreneur, the time to earn an income from the information you already have in your head is now!

Creating your information product

Here are a few examples of the many Information Product formats you can use:

- An e-book or short report. E-books should be at least 30 to 60 pages in length and contain lots of photos or diagrams to create white space on the page and make it easier and more exciting to read; short reports can be as brief as one or two pages, but four to ten pages is an optimum length
- A newsletter
- Computer software
- An information-based webinar
- Audio recordings (typically recorded using the MP3 file format)
- Audio/Visual recordings typically recorded using the AVI, WMV, MPEG, or other file formats

You must exercise some discipline to organize your thoughts and reduce your ideas to writing. The following considerations are critical:

- Give yourself a realistic, time-bound goal that identifies when you would like to generate the first sale of your Information Product
- Identify when, where, and how you like to write or be creative and replicate those circumstances each time you sit down to begin work on your book or product
- Purchase a journal or a voice recorder to capture the ideas as they come up at the time of conception (otherwise, these ideas may become lost forever)

♦ Surround yourself with the sights, sounds, and smells that enhance your creativity and ability to write with comfort and ease;

♦ Discipline your use of time by establishing a regular writing schedule that includes a break every now and then to relax, refresh your thoughts, and replenish your creative batteries

With these basic considerations in mind, it is now time to create your Information Product. Be sure to have an editor or peer reviewer evaluate your product and offer constructive comments. Test marketing is the quickest way to ensure you have a viable product before investing significant resources into a major launch.

Making it digital

In most cases your Information Product will be delivered digitally online. This means the customer receives the product within seconds of purchasing it. Consider some of the resources you can use:

♦ **Adobe Acrobat (full version)** — create Adobe PDF files (e.g., e-books or newsletters) that can be shared across various computer platforms

♦ **GoToWebinar** *(www.gotowebinar.com)* — host online webinars featuring PowerPoint presentations or other online demonstrations, the content of which can be recorded and repackaged into a downloadable Information Product

♦ **Free Conference Call Services** — deliver audio content to a group of listeners; these "teleseminars" can be recorded as MP3 files and sold as a standalone entity or included as part of other Information Products

- **Video Capture Devices (e.g., Camtasia; Flip Video Camera)** — capture presentations on the screen of your computer or create videos of live events that can later be uploaded to your website, YouTube, Facebook, or other video or social media websites

- **Computer Software Programming Language** — write computer software applications, which can later be sold for a profit. Microsoft Windows, Mac computers, and the iPhone are typical target platforms

Establishing your online presence

In chapter 2 we discussed how to register your domain name and create a website to sell your Information Product. I recommend you also register closely related domain names to protect your brand and online identity. In addition, redirecting these other domains to your home page can also drive more traffic to your site.

You will need to apply for a merchant account and choose a payment gateway service provider to enable your website to accept credit cards, electronic checks, or other forms of payment. When possible, consider making your Information Product the only product that is sold on your website (this helps maintain your prospect's focus on your specific product and the exact steps to take to complete the transaction). If this is not possible, then at least have one page on your website dedicated solely to your Information Product.

At a minimum, your website solution should provide:

- A squeeze page, which you use for marketing purposes to acquire names and email addresses of leads (usually for free) in return for offering them something of nominal value. If you wrote an e-book, this is usually where you offer a free downloadable chapter of your book. The last page of the free chapter should contain marketing ad copy that brings them back to your sales page (see below)

♦ A sales page to which your leads (prospects) are directed so they can make a purchase

♦ A shopping cart and payment gateway service provider to accept credit card payments

♦ A merchant account which finalizes the transaction and sends the funds to your business bank account

You may still be asking the question: "How do I monetize this?" Driving traffic to your website as John Limbocker explained in chapter 3 is a great way. However, one of the best (and fastest) ways to monetize a new product or a new business is through the use of joint ventures, which we will cover in the next section.

Leveraging joint ventures to drive massive revenue

If you want more sales, you are a good candidate for a joint venture. To create a joint venture, you simply find another company who is already successful and whose clients are predisposed to purchase what you have to sell. Make sure your product does not compete with their product or service. Ideally your Joint Venture (JV) partner has a large list. Finally, your cost to get into the JV partnership should be a low point of entry.

Here are the top three strategies for creating the best joint ventures.

1. All Joint Ventures should be documented in writing in the form of an agreement.

   • Those agreements not reduced to writing run the risk of falling apart over time with no option for you to claim what may rightfully be yours.

- Furthermore, without a written agreement, it's possible each party to the agreement may have a different perspective of what the compensation plan should be. You don't want to do all the work to get to your first pay day only to argue with your joint venture partner over the percentage he or you were supposed to get.

2. If the JV involves the exchange of your intellectual property (which, in most cases, it will) you should also have a non-exclusive licensing agreement which stipulates the conditions of how the intellectual property will be handled between all parties.

   - Anytime you give permission allowing another party to use your intellectual property, the licensing agreement should spell out the terms of use. A separate Term Sheet can also be used to specify additional terms and conditions that will be applied to the agreement.

   - For example, you may not want your JV Partner to materially transform your intellectual property in any way. If these terms are not spelled out, you may be surprised to find your product appearing in an altered form, in different packaging, or even under a different name. Such alterations of your intellectual property must never be allowed to occur without your knowledge and consent.

   - Always seek a non-exclusive agreement so your opportunities to create other JV relationships remain open.

3. Use a Confidentiality Agreement (CDA) or Non-Disclosure Agreement (NDA) to further protect the confidential Intellectual Property belonging to each of the JV agreement parties.

- The CDA (or NDA) is intended to prevent your JV Partner from exposing your intellectual property to a third party without your permission.

- Part of the CDA will describe what the exceptions are to this type of agreement (e.g., information which is public knowledge or already known by the parties to the agreement at the time the agreement is signed).

Another type of joint venture is often referred to as Affiliate Programs. Under this scenario, the affiliate sends leads or clients in his/her database to a website controlled by the person who has created and manages the affiliate program. Should any of these leads make a purchase while at that website, the revenue is collected by the affiliate program manager and the person who sent the lead (the affiliate) earns a commission on the sale.

In the case of your Information Product, you can establish an affiliate program and invite other individuals to join your program as affiliates. These affiliates can now send their leads/prospects to your website. The percentage per sale you offer your affiliates will vary but it should be enough to readily entice affiliates to join your program while at the same time allowing you to make a decent profit on each sale. Conversely, instead of being the affiliate program manager, you can simply be someone else's affiliate and send members from your own database to someone else's website; now, when each purchase is made, you receive a portion of the profits.

Many people ask, "Where do I find good JV partners?" This is most easily accomplished by networking and constantly letting people know what you are looking for. Not every JV partner you interview will be appropriate for a partnership with your business, so you will want to talk with several new JV prospects each week. Entrepreneurial member-based groups with online forums or regular monthly meetings are also excellent places to locate potential JV partners; you can locate such groups through

Meetup.com. Kerrie Espuga will explain in chapter 13 how you can use Meetup.com to grow your business.

Example

Tom Powers is a real estate investor who has spent the last five years buying residential single-family homes and managing them for a profit (e.g., a consistent 20% return on investment in the initial year alone). One day, while talking about what he does at a networking party, ten people ask him for more information about how he makes money investing in real estate. Realizing what he knows about his greatest skill set (i.e., successfully investing in real estate) can be transformed into something of value, he decides to create a business that helps other beginning real estate investors duplicate the success he has experienced.

Tom spends three months writing a 150-page workbook entitled, "How to Purchase Your First Investment Home and Turn a Profit." The workbook covers such things as: getting organized; how to find your market; how to build your team in that market; typical mistakes investors make; and making your first offer to buy. Once the workbook is created, he spends another two weeks putting together a set of three audio CD's that focus on him teaching the content in the workbook.

He packages it all together and places it on a website, where it can be purchased for $29.95. During this time, he has assembled a list of 200 people who have become interested in what he is doing. He sends out an email to drive these people to his website. Out of those 200 people, 56 people open his message, five people click through to his website, and none of them makes a purchase. Dejected, Tom is about to abandon his business when a friend suggests he talk to a business coach. Deciding to give it one more try, Tom finds a business coach and explains what he wants to do. Tom's business coach looks at his business model and explains what went wrong:

- Tom needs more products in his marketing funnel (up to now, he has built his entire business around a single product)

- The first time prospects enter Tom's marketing funnel, they are being asked to spend $29.95 before they even have an opportunity to know more about what Tom does and how he can help them

- Tom needs a marketing plan designed to generate many leads that can then be marketed to over an extended period of time (typical of most businesses, Tom's prospects will need to hear or see his marketing message five or six times before they are ready to take action)

With this advice Tom goes back to the drawing board. He takes his original 150-page workbook and creates a shortened version of it. He reorganizes this information into a report "How to Avoid the Top Ten Mistakes in Real Estate Investing." This 10-page report is converted into a downloadable PDF file, which he now features on his website's home page. This page now becomes the squeeze page where Tom's prospects will first encounter his marketing message. When arriving at the site, they hear a 30-second audio welcome message from Tom that encourages them to enter their name and email address in exchange for a *FREE* copy of the report that will help them avoid making costly real estate investing mistakes.

Because Tom hired out his website development, he now has the time to expand his marketing funnel. While his website is being built, he creates a plan to promote himself as a keynote speaker on topics involving real estate investing. He believes he can command between $500 and $2500 per speech, depending on the venue, and add back-of-room sales to that total.

Next he realizes his 150-page workbook (the item most people would purchase after hearing him speak or reading his free report) may still not be enough to give people the complete confidence they need to take the first step toward investing in real estate. Tom therefore decides to offer a 1-day boot camp for $895 where he will go into exceedingly greater detail surrounding his workbook, and it will also feature one or two guest speakers as added value. Finally, he sees the opportunity for a flagship product: a 3-day Real Estate Tour to a selected "hot" market, where he could charge $3995 and essentially walk his clients through their first investment property purchase.

There are four real estate investment clubs within a one-hour drive of Tom's house. He contacts the president of each club and creates a joint venture with each of them. If they list him as a preferred trainer and information resource on their website, he will give the investment club a percentage of all sales from that marketing exposure. Tom also knows two personal development speakers who have hundreds of thousands of people in their databases; however, neither of these two speakers offers their clients a real estate investment solution for creating wealth. Tom creates joint ventures with these two speakers by establishing them as affiliates.

Eighteen months after Tom almost quit his business, he now finds himself contacting 2000 new prospects each month and informing them about his business. Approximately 560 of these prospects actually click through to his squeeze page, where 60% of them (336) choose to download his FREE report. Nearly six percent of these individuals purchase his workbook ($29.95) — that's 20 sales monthly for $599.

In addition, Tom delivers a keynote speech eight times a year and averages $4000 per appearance, including back-of-the-room sales. He delivers three boot camps and three real estate tours a year, each of which are attended by five to fifteen people.

Tom is in command of a business grossing more than $125,000 annually, and all of it is built on the pillars of a single Information Product he created and joint ventures he strategically leveraged. The beauty of all this is there is virtually no limit to the ways Tom can continue leveraging his information into new products and/or services he can sell to his clients. Tom's marketing funnel is shown below.

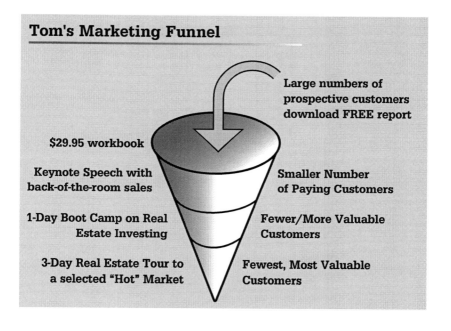

Tom's Marketing Funnel

Large numbers of prospective customers download FREE report

$29.95 workbook

Keynote Speech with back-of-the-room sales

Smaller Number of Paying Customers

1-Day Boot Camp on Real Estate Investing

Fewer/More Valuable Customers

3-Day Real Estate Tour to a selected "Hot" Market

Fewest, Most Valuable Customers

About the author

John C. Robinson is an award-winning author and an in-demand speaker who has shared the stage with Bob Proctor and financial strategist Loral Langemeier. In 1979 John discovered his passion for the world of birds, nature, and the outdoors. Since then, he has written and published six books, led clients on natural history tours around the world, and authored the computer program code for nature-based software which has sold hundreds  *of thousands of copies in the international marketplace. For more resources and information on how to launch an entrepreneurial career using books or other information products, visit www.earnprofitsfromyourpassion.com*

✍   Tip from Shamayah!

Do you wonder where you can find joint ventures? When you are ready to learn, meet, mingle, and create powerful friendships and relationships to grow your business, join the Joint Venture Club at:
www.coauthorswanted.com/jvclub

 # Understanding your target market

Nadia Semerdjieva

Once you know your expertise and how you are going to create your information products, it is vital to research your market. Who is going to buy your products? The answer to this question is very important — you need to know your target market. Once you know this, you can create tailor-made products to fulfill their desires, meet their needs, and solve their problems. Nadia Semerdjieva will explain how to find your target market, and what's more, how to communicate with them in their own language so they will want to buy from you —

— Shamayah

> Talk to people in their own language.
> If you do it well, they'll say,'He said exactly what I was thinking.'And when they begin to respect you, they'll follow you to the death.
>
> — *Lee Iacocca*

Let's say you are playing catch — would you turn around and throw the ball to the nearby tree or just anywhere? Of course not. I'm guessing you would aim the ball toward the catcher's glove. Well, at least if you want him to catch it, that's what you would do. As with anything you want to achieve, you need to aim at your "target."

Suppose you are selling baseballs. You would make more money if you go to places where you can find baseball players than if you try to sell them at a tennis club, right? Of course! This is a very obvious example, yet the same principle applies to the products you are going to create or already have created. You need to be crystal clear on who your target market is. Do you know who your ideal client is?

Finding out exactly what your ideal client looks like is a process that will evolve over time. Where do you start? Well, you put on your detective hat, and you survey your:

+ Past customers

+ Ideal future prospects

+ People you do not want as customers

The next step is to group them. The more detailed you can get, the better. Segment them by gender, age range, income range, family structure, level of education, ethnicity/race, profession, social attitude (e.g., conservative, youthful, collegiate, punk, etc.). The more detailed you get, the better. It's really that important.

Let's do an exercise that will really help you unleash your success:

+ How old is your customer or client? Are they male or female?

+ Where does he/she shop? What time of day are they most likely shopping?

+ What type of food do they like? Do they cook or eat out?

♦ What's their education level? What kind of jobs are they drawn to?

♦ What kind of family life do they lead? With whom do they hang out?

♦ What problems keep them up at night? (This is a BIG one!)

A vision of the person you will target with your marketing message is beginning to take shape. Armed with this information, you now know your ideal client's gender, age group, life style choices, number of kids, car they drive, type of job they have, and whether they are married, widowed, or divorced. Your ideal client may have a name (e.g., "Carine") and ... you may even have a representative picture of her on your desk (yes, nothing like really getting into it ☺).

Thanks to your market research you know exactly what your ideal client's needs are, and with the picture in front of you, you know to whom you are talking when you create your products and marketing materials. The next step is to learn *how* to "talk" to this ideal client. How do you phrase things in a way to help your target market really understand your product is for them?

Speak to your client authentically, from the heart, and in her "own language." You establish rapport this way, because the communication is uncritically accepted by establishing common ground on a subconscious and conscious level. Simply, this means you must talk to them in a way they *get it*. That's why you discovered your target market, so you could learn "their language." There are several different models categorizing the behaviors, styles, preferences, and values of human beings. I've studied this subject for years, and as you can imagine there is a lot to be shared.

To help you get started, I will explain four basic models you can use to communicate more effectively. It may take some practice to apply these models, but keep in mind the better you understand your target market and what drives them, the better your results will be. You will be able to use this information when you meet somebody in person or when you are creating your marketing materials. Believe me, your sales will explode! As you explore "who people are and what makes them tick," you will enter the secret world of your clients and capture their desires much more efficiently. Yes, it also works with the opposite sex and with kids (*that's why I got into it—it was exhausting negotiating with my kids! Soooo much better now!* ☺)

The four basic models are:

1. Motivators of Humankind

2. Inferential and Non-inferential Listeners

3. Favored Representational Systems (as per Advanced Neuro Dynamics)

4. Most Common Business Values

1. Motivators of humankind

What drives us, what motivates us to behave as we do, and how does this motivation work? These questions have been of utmost importance to humankind throughout history. Interestingly, since the dawn of mankind, we have been motivated by the same triggers:

- **Self-preservation** — fear of losing something, survival
- **Gain/Greed** — emotional and/or physical

- **Social Acceptance** — approval of society

- **Higher Group Status** — having the finest, most luxurious things

+ **Love/Sex**—attractiveness to the opposite sex

+ **Duty/Guilt**—helping a downtrodden group

When you understand which one of these motivators is strongest in your target market you can apply those motivators to your sales copy. For example, let's say you offer a product that is only available for a limited number of people. Somebody may fear he will lose something valuable and decide to buy it today. Or, what if you offered a very exclusive retreat for a small, select group of your clients? This will appeal to their "Higher Group Status."

Spiral Dynamics is a model that makes sense of the enormous complexity of human existence and shows how to find solutions that meet people where they are. By exploring and describing the core intelligence and deep values that flow beneath what we believe and do, the model offers a dynamic perspective on complex matters such as:

+ HOW people think about things (as opposed to "what" they think)

+ WHY people make decisions in different ways

+ WHY people respond to different motivators

One reason why I love Spiral Dynamics so much is because it literally zeros in on the ONE motivator which will be most important to your specific client, and it helps explain how to bring it out in them! Can you see the potential? ☺ You could generate specific conversations for healing, selling, understanding one another, negotiating, motivating, etc.

Furthermore, there are four basic, fundamental driving values that tend to excite people:

+ **Recognition**—the acknowledgment of something as valid or as entitled to consideration

+ **Security**—the state of being free from danger or injury;

defense against financial failure; financial independence; freedom from anxiety or fear

+ **Freedom** — the condition of being free; the power to act or speak or think without externally imposed restraints

+ **People/Connections** — an arrangement to execute orders or advance the interests of another

Values such as "Security" and "Freedom" may seem to conflict; however, as you can see in the above definitions, those values can also be phrased in a way to complement each other. When you are working with your target market, you want to consider whether your particular client is seeking those values because of a pull toward or a push away. Furthermore, you want to be clear as to whether your use of any one value in your writing/script/ copy conflicts with another predominant value or complements it.

2. Inferential and non-inferential listeners

Have you ever noticed what you say is not necessarily what someone hears? I guess you are not the only one. The way some people think, they can infer a "conclusion" from what is being said, whereas others cannot. For example, if I say, "I'm cold" — a non-inferential listener would hear just that — a statement of fact that I am cold. Period. On the other hand, an inferential listener would understand that yes, I am cold, AND I desire to be warmer — so she would most likely offer me a jacket or ask if I would like the heat turned up. No, this type of response is not due to social upbringing, although it can be refined through socialization. The truth is, some people simply cannot understand when something is being inferred to them!

So how can you use this in your copy? Well, you could speak to the listener who cannot infer at the risk of boring your inferential listeners. The alternative would be to write or speak inferentially to non-inferential listeners and completely lose them. Having said that, if you know your target market well enough, you may be able to deduce which one of the two listening methods is more predominant amongst your clients.

3. Favored Representational Systems (as per advanced neuro dynamics)

We take in and process information through our five senses. We have preferred ways of doing this — visually, auditorily, kines-thetically, and through our taste and smell. Your preferred way of processing is called your Favored Representational System. When you know your own and your ideal clients' Favored Representational System, you will understand what kind of language appeals to them. When people have the same representational system or if they are using words that are in ours we find them more likeable or appealing, because subconsciously "we talk the same language."

There are four Favored Representational Systems I want to share with you. Even though each person has a primary and secondary one, all of the representational systems contribute to the overall absorption of information within a person:

Visual

People who are visual often stand or sit with their heads and/or bodies erect, with their eyes up. They usually breathe from the top of their lungs. They tend to sit forward in their chair and tend to be organized, neat, well groomed, and orderly. They are often thin and wiry. They memorize by seeing pictures, and are less distracted by noise. They often have trouble remembering verbal instructions because their minds tend to wander. A visual person will be interested in how your program LOOKS. Appearances are important to them.

So, what does that all mean? In order to captivate your visual clients, you want to communicate using visual cues, words, and phrases such as:

+ "See"

+ "Check this out"

+ "Take a look at this"

+ Write as if you are describing a picture — colors, near or far, moving or still, etc.

+ Use sight oriented words such as shiny, glossy, see-through, crumpled, etc.

+ Have a video playing

+ A webinar will be much better for them than a teleconference

Auditory

People who are auditory will often move their eyes sideways. They breathe from the middle of their chest. They typically talk to themselves (some even move their lips when they talk to themselves). They can be easily distracted by noise. They can repeat things back to you easily, they learn by listening, and usually like music and talking on the phone. They memorize by steps, procedures, and sequences (sequentially). The auditory person likes to be told how they are doing, and responds to a certain tone of voice or set of words. They will be interested in what you have to SAY about your program!

Thus, in order to captivate your auditory clients, you want to:

+ Have music playing

+ Have teleconferences (instead of long web pages that go on for miles)

♦ Have a video playing—there is still sound there. Pay attention, though, to what tonality is used in the video

♦ Describe things as if you are describing a song—loud or soft, tonality, timbre, pauses, etc.

♦ Use sound-oriented words such as quiet, deafening, shrill, thunderous, screeching

Kinesthetic

People who are kinesthetic will typically breathe from the bottom of their lungs, so you will see their stomach go in and out when they breathe. They often move and talk *verrrry slooooowly*. They respond to physical rewards, and touching. They also stand closer to people than a visual person does. They memorize by doing or walking through something. They will be interested in your program if it "feels right," or if you can give them something they can grasp.

With kinesthetic people, you want to allow them to experience things through your words (i.e., they are more attracted to hands-on things, workshops, retreats, etc.):

♦ Use touch-oriented words such as smooth, sandy, warm, heavy, sticky

♦ Describe the shape, size, weight or pressure

♦ Talk about actions such as going, playing, running, lifting

Auditory digital

Persons with this representational system spend a fair amount of time talking to themselves. They will want to know if your program "makes sense." The auditory digital person can exhibit characteristics of the other major representational systems. This person is much more analytical and likes systems, sequences, and patterns. They are usually slower to process things and tend to repeat things several times. They tend to be non-inferential listeners.

To connect with an Auditory Digital person, you want to allow them to:

- Understand things

- Understand the value

- See, hear, or get that it makes sense (depending on what other major representational system is involved)

- Organize things, events, and information sequentially, methodically, and clearly

- Perceive things linearly — think how you would talk to an engineer (I can say that — both of my parents are engineers, and I LOVE them!)

> If you talk to a man in a language he understands, that goes to his head. If you talk to him in his language, that goes to his heart.
>
> — *Nelson Mandela*

4. Most common values in a business person today

Since we cannot explore all the different Personalities and Styles in this chapter, let's focus on Orange Level Values as per Spiral Dynamics (similar to the Competitive Persona) — the most predominant business person today. Understanding just the basics of Orange Level Values can explode your current business.

The Orange Level Person will be intrigued by trial-and-error experiments where success brings anticipated gains; competitive gaming with high-tech, high status tools, and prestigious experts. Thus, if your ideal client has a Competitive Persona, you want to showcase your experts and talk about opportunities for success and competitive advantage.

Imagine you are motivating a Competitive Persona — your copy will succeed with:

♦ "Be the first to get there!"

♦ "The first five sign-ups will receive a free night in Maui!"

♦ "Only a few make it to the Platinum Inner circle, will you be one of them?"

♦ "Are you tired of your old ___, be the first to get the new and improved __"

Hmmmm, what would entice an Orange Level? What kind of "job" will capture their interest? Here is what they would say about their perfect job: "I like a job where successful performance advances my career. I get ahead and reach my goals. I am well-compensated and my work priorities are determined by my results and career plan."

The Orange Level or Competitive Persona IS the enterprising self — the, materialist who expresses herself to make her life better! Let's call her "Carine." Her operating system is based on experimenting with change and entrepreneurial alternatives to reach her goals and to improve herself and others. There is no "it's just how things are" — the focus is on "always better." Her learning style is one of expectancy — trial and error experiments where success brings anticipated gains, competitive gaming with high-tech, high status tools, and prestigious experts. Translated into usable knowledge — let her know how your product/service is high-tech, and what kind of experts you have to take her to the next level in her career - Easy! ☺

Carine's management style is Economic — competitive and

goal-oriented with perks for winners and rewards measured by productivity, political savvy, contribution, or entrepreneurial skills. She wants to be recognized as an expert herself (and usually people like her are great experts). So, Carine's motivational hot buttons are:

♦ Opportunities for success

♦ Progress and competitive advantage

♦ Prestige

♦ Bigger and better, or new and improved

What do you think Carine's motivator is as we talked about in section I? You got it—**"Higher Group Status."**

You get the subtle flare of this focus? If your ideal client is an Orange Level, Competitive Persona, apply this in your marketing materials, services, and product. Talk their language, offer them value based on what they want (the high tech, high status, prestigious experts) and transform your business into a cash machine with lots of happy and satisfied customers ☺.

In closing

You could have a blog, a landing page, and an article for each "type" of client. This would allow you to have a very broad funnel and you would be able to bring in clients representing each of the characteristics I mentioned before. If you don't choose that path, remember you will need to find a common ground that will connect with almost everyone. You want to ensure the words you use appeal and create rapport with all types. Take the information and apply it in your blogs, articles, etc., for great results.

Knowing your clients will allow you to connect better with them, because you can talk "the same language." It also allows you to spice up your communication by using descriptive words for the different representational systems. If you know who your ideal clients are, focus most of your efforts on creating an absolutely irresistible offer, specifically designed for them! As you learn and utilize this information in your videos, blogs, articles, and books, your conversion rates will increase, your articles will be read more often, and people will simply want to follow you on Twitter. You can even use it in ordinary conversations (yes, it can make a difference even with your kids — believe me, I know).

I sincerely hope you will visit me at:

www.leadingfrominspiration.com

About the author

Nadia Gueorguieva Semerdjieva has been trained in numerous modalities addressing the Conscious and Subconscious mind. Having graduated second in her Economics class and graduated Summa Cum Laude from Boston University's Business School, Nadia went on to receive her Masters in Intellectual Property and a Law Degree. Today, Nadia enjoys combining all of her knowledge to help businesses better understand their clients and employees, and thus create a synergistic,  *win/win, harmonious environment that yields immediate results in productivity, client retention, and team work!*

 **Tip from Shamayah!**

Understanding individual differences and being able to communicate effectively starts with gaining more insight into the strengths and challenges of your own personality and behavioral style. Learn more about yourself and take your assessment at: **www.coauthorswanted.com/assessment**

 # Your social media success formula

Meredith Collins

Once you understand your target market and you have a clear picture of who your ideal clients or customers are, you will know where they can be found — and very likely, they will be online. Social media and social networking have become a very popular and successful way to connect, find solutions for problems, or simply know what is going on. Many journalists are using social media to find news or interesting stories. Ninety percent of all people will "Google it" before they ever make contact with a business. Does your business have a powerful Internet presence? If not, you're about to discover social media is an outstanding way to create a powerful Internet presence, that is, if you know how to do it right. But where do you start? Meredith Collins will explain how to be successful in social networking. This is very valuable information, because once you have the knowledge and learn the skills you need to properly use social media — your possibilities are limitless!

— Shamayah

> I collect human relationships very
> much the way others collect fine art.
> — *Jerzy Kosinski*

Relationships are very important in social marketing. This is one aspect of human behavior that has not changed in thousands of years—the basic human need to belong. Wanting to be part of a tribe, to be connected, and to feel valuable are innate human needs. The social networks, both on- and offline, to which you belong, are simply an extension of these theories of human connectedness—they are about belonging in the millennium.

Social networking (and marketing) = building relationships + trust = sales

All social networking is built on the premise of building relationships, trust, and adding value, thus positioning yourself and your business as trusted, valuable, and the expert. This is often a difficult concept for small business owners and entrepreneurs to grasp as we are often driven by the need to make a sale. However, in social networking, the sale follows the relationship building. This can take a while to develop, or it can happen very quickly.

With basic social media tools, you can tap into markets that may not have previously been available to you—all with minimal marketing costs. If, however, you are a smaller enterprise and locally based, social media gives you the opportunity to effectively reach your market through a different channel and add to your marketing arsenal. Social media is exciting and is a worthwhile investment for your effort—and the only cost to you and your business is the time you invest in updating the content.

Several key considerations can easily help you decide what you should be doing in social media:

+ You can look at your competitors' websites and critique them. Do they use social media? How many followers or friends do they have? What are they doing well? Become their follower or friend, sign up for their blog, and research what they are doing.

♦ What is your Unique Selling Proposition (USP) — What makes you unique and why do people choose your business? Carry that theme into your social media. Don't create mixed messages for your market. Keep clarity around your business, your USP, and what your market wants.

♦ Check other social media pages, such as Facebook Business Pages, Twitter, and LinkedIn and see what makes a good profile stand out from one that isn't so good. Your profile needs to be complete, look good, and soundly represent you and your business. We offer Social Media Health Checks, because bad profiles are just that — bad!

♦ Always keep your target market in mind. As Nadia Semerdjieva recommended in chapter 8, keep a picture of your ideal client on your desk. What is his or her profile? They are most likely playing in social spaces. Knowing your target market means you can better meet their problems and needs! Their profile and demographic will determine which social sites will most likely appeal to them.

♦ Decide what it is you want to achieve through social networking. Do you want to:

  • Add customers and clients who will buy your existing products?

  • Add new customers who will buy new products and services?

  • Retain the same customers and add revenue to each sale?

  • Retain the same customers but add new products to existing markets?

♦ Is your product or service sold business to business, business to consumer, or both?

♦ Are you a solopreneur (with some time once a day or week)

or do you have a person who can work this marketing method for you on a regular basis?

♦ What is your market looking for: information, offers or promotions, how to, or education? How will you best serve your market using social media marketing?

♦ How much time can you dedicate to this process? Do you know which sites/opportunities will give you the most value?

♦ Finally, how are you branding yourself? Brand equity is critical. Whenever you set up a Facebook Page, blog, or other Social Media profile, ensure your brand is consistent. For example, when a customer moves from your profile on one social network site to your blog or website, it should be clear they all belong to you.

With answers to all these considerations you may find your strategy will begin to appear. Remember, this is about relationship building. You don't go to a party and sell someone the first time you meet. Instead, you build a relationship; discuss what you do, what they do, what you like, what they like, your hobbies, and so forth. From this initial conversation, you move into a position where you have rapport and the opportunity to offer solutions to their needs. Face to face, this process takes some time. In social networking, it can happen very quickly! Be prepared to be tenacious in building this presence.

We need to go to the masses, and when we do, we need to be armed with a marketing funnel that offers them great value, positions you as an expert, and begins the process of creating relationships you can eventually monetize. Your strategy for marketing must be clear and focused.

Your marketing funnel is important

In order to begin developing your relationships and increasing your attractiveness to your target audience, your marketing funnel needs to be in place. In chapter 6 Erica Lewis explained how to create your marketing funnel. Loral Langemeier compares this with the dating game. The top of your funnel is like going on a first date where you and your prospect are both testing the waters. A well designed marketing funnel will make customers enter your database—and a properly managed database is gold. As you review your marketing funnel, ask these basic questions:

◆ What is free or of minimal cost to you but valuable to your prospects? In other words, what might they want or need and be willing to exchange their valuable contact information for? This is often a "free gift"—and your "free gift" must be descriptive, such as a report, a special video, or maybe a chapter of your book (first date).

◆ What is your "first sell"—a higher cost item that builds trust and rapport (going steady)?

◆ What can you up sell and use to continue to develop the relationship (engaged)?

◆ How can you maintain an ongoing relationship with them (get married)?

The bigger question becomes, "How does my business convey this through social media?" If social media is to fully take the place of a website (and it can), then you must keep in mind social media is about relationships; but what other information is required? Well, a blog, integrated into Facebook, with a LinkedIn profile can be very effective. Consider the following:

◆ Does your social media strategy give your target market what it wants? Does it tell them clearly what to do next?

For example, if you want them to opt in to receive your e-book, is that call to action clearly displayed the moment they hit your site?

♦ Is your landing page and/or video effective? Does it convey the right message?

♦ Can they easily opt in to your database via your Facebook site, blog, website, or other opt-in portal?

♦ Does your website allow them to build rapport and develop a relationship with you and your business?

♦ Are your social media accounts and your website branded effectively and consistently?

You may also want to contribute to and develop a following on a niche site pertaining to your business and area of expertise. These sites are specialized, and people looking for information on your industry or business will go to these sites to gather information. You can then link these sites back to your main social media site.

In sum, marketing is a critical business function. The time spent creating, implementing, monitoring, evaluating, and tweaking your marketing message is worth every penny. Creating an online social media following requires three things: time, tenacity, and execution of your marketing strategy.

Is there a formula?

Some say the magic formula is Twitter + Facebook + LinkedIn + a niche networking site. Others claim it is Facebook+blog + Twitter+article marketing. For some businesses, it may be as simple as a Facebook page for business OR a blog. My advice is to create leverage at every opportunity. For instance, a Wordpress blog will integrate into a LinkedIn profile and can also be integrated into Facebook — so every time you write a post, it will update your Facebook and LinkedIn profiles automatically. Your formula will ultimately be based on your business, your market, your marketing strategy, and your goals. When choosing your formula, ensure you have the expertise to maintain the formula and dedicate enough time to do so. Maintaining social networks takes time. If you can't create one good quality site of great value, don't create four bad, poor quality ones just so customers will see your business has a profile. Clearly decide which sites and options will create the most value for you and your business.

There are two aspects to consider in developing a social media strategy. The first is the actual mechanics of creating a following, which touches on the posts, the profile, making videos, and more. The second aspect is developing relationships and adding value, which we have looked at earlier.

Getting started — things to remember

Find the media that appeal to you and work for your business — then learn to use them. Mere dabbling in social media does not work and profiles left untouched and incomplete will just hurt your reputation and prevent you from presenting a cohesive, polished, and professional image to your market. Start small. It's best to concentrate your efforts in one area, grow your presence, and then (and only then) move to the next area.

Video is a great option to build your brand and personalize your business for your market like Nohra Leff explained in chapter 5. Video builds rapport with a disparate market more quickly than anything else. Some people may say, "I can't do that" or "I hate the camera" — this isn't about you being a newsreader. People can tell, expect, and accept the difference between a broadcast quality video and a simple video of an individual online discussing a new product, service, or concept. Video is a highly accepted part of social networking and it's worth investigating its application in your business. Remember the old adage, "if you build it, they will come" doesn't work in social networking. Just because you build profiles through these social networking sites doesn't mean people will automatically want to know more about your business. Unless you nurture your web presence and give more than you get, at least initially, you won't develop the following you want.

How much time can you or a member of your team afford to put into social marketing?

This time has to be non-negotiable and a core function of your marketing efforts. Once your profiles are set up, a few hours a week will probably be adequate. It is important to stay focused on your outcome and your goals. Anyone who uses social networking can tell you, it's easy to become completely absorbed and hours disappear! Using an egg timer to control the time spent can be a great idea to keep on task — when the timer goes off, so do you. Whatever you do, discipline is critical so other core functions don't move off the radar! Marketing and sales is a critical part of your business, but not at the expense of other core functions.

What traits should I exercise in using social media?

You have information and knowledge others want and need — develop your reputation and look forward to reaching your audience. As you do so, keep in mind nothing is as important in social marketing as your reputation. Protect it like you would protect your children or loved ones! If your reputation is damaged, you will be in trouble because recovering your reputation is often next to impossible!

Remember, what is posted on the Internet stays on the Internet, even when pages are removed. There is little that cannot be found again. The following five points are very important for developing and maintaining your valuable reputation whilst establishing valuable connections.

1. **Be comfortable in your own skin.** Know who you are and what you offer. Be secure in your position as an expert in your field.

2. **Transparency** — be open with your audience. People like knowing what you are doing and how you are doing it. Share what needs to be shared to entice, interest, and engage and they'll learn to trust you.

3. **Be positive for positive results.** By conveying positive news and helpful information, you will be someone people want to interact with.

4. **Have faith in building relationships and your reputation.** A week won't do it; possibly a month won't either. So be patient and let it happen. You've got to let social networking play out, and then take a look at your business in a year. It is going to be tremendously different compared to where it is right now.

5. **Contribute and converse at least every other day!** Get involved in the conversation and be willing to give as much as (or even more than) what you're getting in return. This will quickly grow your reputation. Work to position yourself as an expert in a specific task or specific industry. This means sharing your knowledge, building your reputation, and eventually, the money will come.

How can you contribute to different forums and groups?

If somebody has a question, be one of the first people to answer without any sort of a sell attached. Don't tell them to buy your book: just answer their question. They will find your products if you give them value and scratch their itch. Give people your input and encourage them to get better at what they are trying to do.

> I am a little pencil in the hand of a writing God who is sending a love letter to the world.
>
> — *Mother Teresa*

The unspoken rules of social networking

In creating a following, there are a few simple rules of Netiquette to follow. Break these cardinal rules, and you will forever be banished! They are simple and common sense — although often broken by those chasing a quick buck. Breaking social networking rules is what spamming is to e-mail!

1. **Never include a direct link to a squeeze page or sales letter via social networking.** Anything you promote needs to be wrapped in value-added content offered to your prospects.

2. **Never give your market any reason not to trust you.** This means only send quality, valuable information and never send junk.

3. **Do not be a sales geek.** Never EVER pitch or sell in the first instance. Remember, this is like the person at the party who tries to sell you something even though he or she doesn't know you. Nor should you invite people to be part of your network and immediately leave a pitch on their site when they accept your invitation. Hard selling is not part of the

social media marketing space. Use a softer sell and you will find your relationship with the market becomes aligned to your brand.

4. **Understand the concept of privacy.** Privacy and social networking do not belong in the same sentence. You must be careful about what you are posting and what you are willing to have on the Internet. There is a fine line between building relationships and keeping to the business end of things. If you wouldn't share the information at a face-to-face networking event, don't share it online.

5. **Be visible.** So, you haven't lost the 20 kg or had the Botox you've been threatening! It's okay. It's about being human, visible, and warm. If potential clients discriminate based on the way you look, who wants to work with them anyway!

6. **Walk the controversial line with care.** It's true, being a little controversial or making contentious statements can cause a stir and create interest. It can also split your market. You may make a statement that is neither right nor wrong and is merely "personal opinion." But if the statement causes 50 percent of your market to dismiss you because you have made a comment about politics, race, religion, or abortion, it's potentially a big price to pay. So, if you are going to make contentious statements, think carefully about your market's perception and not only how it can add interest, but how it can detract from what you want to achieve.

7. **Don't use the space to be frivolous or goofy.** If you are using the social space for business marketing, be aware of the message you send if you are "poking" someone on Facebook, twittering nonsense, or not adding value. Have some fun by all means and be witty and clever, but stick to the

ethos of your business. For instance, I don't get involved in "Farmville," "Mafia Games," or other activities like that on Facebook. I am also careful of what images I post; and although I share "life information" on my personal profile, there is nothing my clients of Video.Social.Marketing have seen or could see I would be ashamed of.

8. **On inviting others to connect with you.** If you know someone personally or have met them, by all means send them an automated connection invite. If you have never met them personally, or the relationship is distant, out of courtesy, write a short note explaining why you would like to connect and how you are connected. This is courteous and your invitation is far less likely to be ignored, especially if people are looking to create meaningful connections.

Reap the rewards

Approaching social media marketing as a business activity that can be fun and very satisfying will really help you connect with others and expand your customer base — and that's exciting! Social media networking is really about building relationships. Dollars will come when you are of service to others. Connecting with and helping people will pay off. People will become loyal followers of what you do and, in turn, recommend you.

Serving, giving not taking, delivering massive value, and having a solid presence and security in who you are and what you and your business stand for — all of these are critical aspects to being able to monetize your marketing efforts, both on- and offline. Social media marketing using social media, networking, and video requires an investment of your time and probably a change in your business mindset. The rewards can be outstanding. Your interaction with a global community has the potential to change the face of your business — are you ready?

The content of this chapter was current when the book was written. Technology continues to develop, so please visit my website to find the latest information.

About the author

Meredith Collins has many years of experience in social networking and social media, having been an eLearning consultant and mentor for a major College network in NSW, Australia. Meredith now specializes in implementing, supporting, and maintaining social media for businesses and is active on the main social networks. Honing her many skills and  knowledge accumulated over the years, she founded the company www.videosocialmarketing.net

 # Turn Facebook friends into customers

Meredith Collins

"I'll send you a friend request on Facebook." You may have heard this sentence more than once. Are you on Facebook already? You may have set up an account and have some friends, but did you know Facebook is a fantastic tool to grow your business and generate traffic to your website? Meredith Collins will show you step by step how you can set up a Facebook Business Page allowing you to stay in touch with your clients, attract new ones, or turn your Facebook friends into clients. You can also join groups to research your target market. Best of all, it is a fun way to market your business and make new friends! —

— Shamayah

> Friends are angels who lift our feet when
> our wings have trouble remembering how to fly.

Facebook was initially a social network set up to help ex-college students find old friends. Today it is much more than that. However, the information you find below is NOT about "friends," "socializing", or finding old college buddies—we are looking at Facebook as a business tool. Personal social profiles are completely separate from Business Pages or Fan Pages. To set the context for Facebook Business Pages, here are some facts about the fastest growing social network:

♦ Facebook has 400 million active users and this is growing exponentially

♦ The average user:

- Has 130 friends on the site and sends eight friend requests per month

- Spends more than 55 minutes per day on Facebook

- Writes 25 comments on Facebook content sites each month

- Becomes connected to or "Likes" three Pages and is invited to three events per month

- Is a member of 12 groups

♦ The fastest growing demographic on Facebook is women over 35, followed closely by women over 55

♦ The largest represented demographic is currently the age group 18-29, followed closely by the age group 30-34

What does this mean for business?

"Veterans" (those born prior to 1946) or "Gen Z" (those born after 1995) are playing on the Social Networking periphery and every other generation is heavily using social networking spaces.

This means even the Veterans or Gen Z are there by proxy — their caregivers, and people helping to make buying decisions for these two generations, are using social networking. Another consideration is your business may, in some way, educate or prepare one generation to become the generation your product or service serves. Around 50% of all Facebook users earn more than $60,000 (U.S.) per year. (Note: these statistics are U.S. based; however, my experience indicates other western cultures are well represented by the U.S. trends.)

What types of pages are available?

Profiles — personal

Your profile allows you to share your interests, activities, and anything else you want with people you connect with on Facebook. Your Facebook profile is about representing yourself and sharing what's going on in your life with your friends; although, to administer a Business Page, you don't need to complete the profile in detail. To set up a Business Page, you must first have set up a personal profile. Many business owners make the mistake of setting up their business as a personal profile — this violates Facebook's Terms of Business. When this happens, Facebook has the right to (and will) take down the Profile without any notice or warning.

Pages — business pages

Pages are used by organizations, businesses, celebrities, authors, and bands to broadcast great information in an official, public manner. Like profiles, they can be enhanced with applications or tabs that help your business or entity communicate with and engage people; likewise, they can capture new audiences virally through their Connections' recommendations to their friends. To create and manage a Page for your organization, you must do so from your personal account. Under the Terms of Business, only an official representative of an organization, business, celebrity, author, or band is permitted to create a Page on behalf of the business or organization. We recommend ensuring your Page is consistent with your branding and message; and promotes and builds relationships in line with your Unique Selling Proposition (USP).

Groups

Groups focus less on a person, brand, or business and more on a shared interest. Unlike Pages, Groups have a 5000-member limit. Groups stand alone as opposed to tying into your brand or USP. Pages tend to work better for businesses while Groups do well for non-profits, interest groups, and causes. A Group can be likened to a "Club" in the offline world.

Considerations before setting up a business page

It is important to note the beauty of a Page is its structured, uncluttered format. It is, however, your responsibility to be creative while customizing your Page to maximize your social networking opportunities. This is best done with the assistance and services of a Facebook Markup Language (FBML) programmer, such as the services we offer.

Facebook's strengths (i.e., its structured, uncluttered format) can also be its downside: Facebook has many anomalies, and its page restrictions can cause frustration for the user. It is a dynamic site with changes occurring frequently. As users, we need to work within the parameters offered, and use artistic license to create added flexibility whenever possible.

How do I set up my business page?

Step 1. Creating your business page

Once you set up your personal profile, at the bottom of the Facebook login page, there is a link on the right side of the page that reads "Create a Page." Once this link is clicked, an options page will appear with a wizard to take you through setting up your Business Page.

Pick the business category best fitting what you will promote. You may not find a perfect fit for your business, but choose the closest match since you won't be able to change your category later. You may need to choose "Other Business" and begin building your Page from there.

The name you give your Page is permanent, so make sure it is easy to recognize. Note: The first goal for your Page (beyond publishing) is to reach 25 Connections — then you can apply for a "Vanity URL" or short URL. Choosing a good name now for your Page is very important to get Connections. Finally, make sure you tick the box to keep the Page unpublished until you have completed it. If this button is unavailable, click "Edit Page" under your logo, go to the "Settings" button, and ensure the Page is only visible by Admin, until you are ready to publish.

Step 2. Populating your Page

Uploading a profile picture is a good place to start because the most important image or photo is the profile picture Facebook users will see (as a thumbnail) in "News Feed" when their friends interact with you. We suggest you use your logo, business premises, or even a group photo of your staff. We recommend this image is one people automatically identify as being your business or organization. Make sure the image is still clear and displays properly when reduced to thumbnail size. Start with a square image and this will make it more likely to display on the Wall correctly (the "Wall" is a space on every user's profile page allowing friends to post messages for the user to see).

You can now click "Add information to this page" underneath the profile picture and enter as much basic and detailed information as you can. The fields available will depend on your Page type. The more details you can add about who you are, what you do, and when and where customers can buy your products, the more successful you will be.

Step 3. Choosing your tabs

Like user profiles, Pages have multiple tabs. Depending on the business type you choose, you will receive default tabs, which can be changed and added to. However, you will receive the following tabs no matter which page type you choose:

- Wall tab for you and your Connections to share content
- Info tab for you to share business information

Without any additional programming, you can add the fairly standard Facebook tabs, such as:

- Links

- Events

- Photos

- Notes

- Videos and more

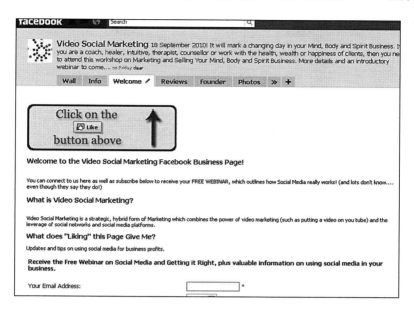

Businesses also have the ability to program their own tabs using FBML. This application, known as Static FBML, shows up as a "Boxes" tab and needs to be programmed and edited. I use this application to create custom landing pages for all my clients, and highly recommend you do the same for your own business.

♦ Custom landing or opt-in page tab (with an appropriate call to action)

Other possible tabs available using Static FBML:

♦ About

♦ Testimonials

♦ Team

♦ Other useful information (particularly in the absence of a formal business website)

We also recommend your Business Page integrates a Blog into its tabs, giving you the opportunity to write longer posts, which adds value for your Connections and continues to feed your Wall.

Businesses use a variety of static (informational) tabs and tabs that are dynamic and update to the Wall, such as photos and videos. This combination of features will continue to regularly add visual interest and rich content to your Page.

Step 4. Add useful and engaging content

Ensure your Page always has some good information about your business. You can do this by adding photos or videos, or other content that enriches the site and creates interest. You can even add more information later—that's the beauty of Facebook. It's a contiually changing web presence.

Step 5. Publish the Page

Click the "Publish this Page" link or change the settings to share your Page with the world. This is your website where your business has a public profile with the power to let your Connections or customers engage their friends on your behalf. You can optimize your Page's performance by clicking the "Edit Page" or "Settings" link to adjust a variety of controls. For example, you can control the default landing tab for users who are not yet Connections of your Page—this is where the custom landing pages come into play and call potential Connections to action.

When you really think about it, someone opting in to become a Connection and "LIKE" your business effectively gives you permission to send out (via your Wall) good quality, meaningful content that lands on their Wall. Once this happens, their 130 friends can now see that good quality, meaningful information. It's almost the new form of email and database marketing. By allowing your Connections to contribute to and share in your Wall posts, photos, and more, your Page will be enriched with Connection interaction and this will support and increase its reach across Facebook.

Step 6. Update regularly

Generally, we encourage clients to update their Page at least two times each week. You want to have fresh content going out regularly. If you have a few Wall posts and a Blog feeding into the site, you can create interest and momentum without being intrusive, in our experience. You don't want your Page to be static and just "sit." Updating your Page regularly with fresh photos, upcoming events, and the latest promotions means visitors will keep coming back.

Facebook users have the option to receive information sorted by what happened most recently. To stay in front of your audience, you want your Page to reflect multiple posts each week. Utilizing modern technology such as mobile phones and related applications, you will find keeping your Page active is easier now than ever before. You will also discover your Connections will be more engaged and more interactive.

How do I find people to connect with my business page?

Good quality, meaningful, and interesting content is king — especially if you want to find and keep Connections for the long term. When managed properly, these Connections will interact with your Page and create a viral marketing impact for your business.

There are a number of ways to find Connections. However, if you don't want to spend any money advertising your Page, there are still several ways to acquire Connections:

1. Use the "Suggest to Friends" link under the profile picture. You can utilize your existing friend connections to suggest to people they "Like a business" (yours, in this case). If they do not respond to the suggestion, then you cannot ask them again — Facebook has been very careful to ensure spam-like activity does not take place with Business Pages.

2. Ask people who use your business and services to "Like" your business. They may be very happy to support and endorse your business while connecting with you on your Business Page.

3. Add a Facebook logo and "call to action" on your website and at the bottom of your emails. Many busi-

nesses use the "Find us on Facebook" logo on their website to advertise the fact they have a Business Page on Facebook.

If you have a budget available, it is possible to advertise your Business Page. If you know your target market, you can give this information to Facebook (along with your budget). Facebook will then advertise your business to your target market using a pay per click strategy within the budget constraints you specify.

Remember, initially, 25 Connections is the magic number. Once you've acquired 25 Connections, you can apply for a custom or vanity URL, which is short and easier to find than the long, ugly URL you typically get by default.

Groups and Business Pages

People using Facebook for business often ask, "Should I have a Business Page or a Group?" Many people suggest you should do both. However, if your time to manage your Facebook content is limited, it is probably a good idea to choose one to start with. Ultimately, the actual solution you choose will depend upon your market and what you are looking to achieve.

The information below should clarify the differences between a Group and a Business Page. We rarely advise our clients to use a Group over a Business Page unless they have a very specific focus or reason.

Why choose a Page over a Group?

Business Page	Group
Business Pages are indexed by Google	Groups are not indexed by Google
When someone finds your Facebook Page from outside of Facebook, they can see the full page and all the information even if they are not logged in—this is why it can act as a website.	To find your Group, someone must be logged into Facebook.
While a Page is created via your personal profile, the two are not linked, which makes it easy to keep professional and personal pages separate if you prefer.	Groups are linked to your personal profile. ■ Positively, you can invite personal connections to join a group you create. ■ Negatively, it can become difficult to separate your personal and professional profiles because the group will also be attached to your personal profile. This can reflect negatively on you if people "misbehave" within the Group.
A Page is completely wide open; anyone who finds the Page can join.	Groups offer the administrator more control over who can join.
If you are using your Facebook Page as your website or primary means of communication, you will not want people's access restricted; although if you don't want someone as a Connection, you can remove them.	Groups can have one of three statuses: ■ Completely open—anyone can join, ■ They can be open but members must first be approved by the administrator, ■ Secret—only those who have been specifically invited will know the group exists.

Business Page	Group
Ability to customize the Page (you can have a Page serve as your website)	Limited ability to customize a Group Page beyond general Facebook tab offerings.
Once a Page has 25 Connections, you may apply for a "vanity URL". This improves the Page's promotional ability and makes it easier to find, for example: *www. Facebook.com/videosocial- markeing* or *www.Facebook. com/yourname*. This appears more professional and is much more likely to improve your SEO.	Groups cannot have a vanity URL so you always have a long and ugly, Facebook-generated URL.
Unlimited number of Connections allowed and posting always takes place via the Wall or other dynamic tabs (i.e., photos, events, etc.). This update will show on their Feed.	Limited to 5000 members and members can be emailed directly from the Group. This message will appear in their Inbox.
A Page can utilize Facebook ads (a paid feature)	A Group can utilize Facebook ads (a paid feature)

What are my options for setting up and maintaining my Business Page?

Make sure your Page is set up properly and professionally. Most business people don't set up their own website; and those who do often have substandard results. Having your Page set up correctly means FBML pages, such as a custom landing tab, at the very least can be incorporated and you have the ability to optimize the Facebook Page. Additionally, there are different areas of a Facebook Page that are indexed by Google, and having a professional set up your Page ensures these aspects will be utilized and implemented, giving you a better result.

Alternatively, you can set the Page up yourself, as we have outlined and demonstrated here. Many of our clients set up their own Page and we then do the programmed tabs. If you have knowledge of HTML (Internet language) then you will be able to program tabs. We recommend posting approximately two to three times per week, or as often as your business and clients dictate. There is also the option of having someone maintain your site for you, as we do for many clients. We briefly talk to them or have email conversations; and for a modest monthly fee, we maintain the Facebook Page and link it to other social media sites, such as Twitter.

Conclusion

Facebook can be a very powerful business tool. As with all marketing strategies, it must be implemented and utilized consistent with your business' market position and brand. All too often I see business owners appear confused about what they want to achieve; and a confused business will lead to confused customers. Well thought out and executed strategies in social networking and Facebook will see your business reap rewards and develop a customer base that is interactive and interested in what you do. I have developed a video that will teach you "How to Get Traffic with Social Media." You can get it for free at *http://www. videosocialmarketing.net*

The content of this chapter was current when the book was written. Technology continues to develop, so please visit my website to find the latest information.

About the author

Meredith Collins' mission is to educate and work with small to medium businesses to implement a social media strategy and optimize their marketing avenues.  *She strives to ensure the social media being utilized are optimized and targeting the appropriate market. Meredith holds qualifications in Marketing, eLearning, Adult Education, Neuro Linguistic Programming, and Management Communications — all of which are very useful when working with your market and social media.*

http://www.videosocialmarketing.net

You can tweet for cash

Terza Ekholm

In April 2008 James Buck, a journalism student from the University of California-Berkeley, was arrested in Egypt while covering an anti-government protest. On his way to the police station, he used his cell phone to send a message to his followers on Twitter — "Arrested." Within seconds, colleagues in the U.S. and his blogger-friends in Egypt — the same ones who taught him the tool only a week earlier, were informed. They alerted the U.S. embassy and his college, which hired a lawyer on his behalf. Within 24 hours, James was released. As he left the station he reached into his pocket to send another one-word message: "Free."

I'm not saying your life depends on using Twitter, but this example shows the power of your network and how technology can help you connect with it. In most cases, Twitter is used in less urgent situations. You can use Twitter to update friends and family. However, if you want to know how you can use this high-tech, low-cost tool to interact with customers, reach new markets, and increase sales, then let me introduce you to Terza Ekholm —

— Shamayah

> Some people come into our lives and quickly go, some stay for a season and say goodbye; they leave their footprints in our hearts, and we are never, ever the same.

Twitter is a social medium that allows you to join the largest party in the world. It's anywhere and everywhere and lasts 24 hours a day. Twitter is fun. Twitter is now. Twitter is annoying and it's social, but can you make any money with it? Businesses of all sizes all over the world participate in this extraordinary medium for marketing, sales, recruiting, feedback, support, or just to connect. If you want to partake of business online in any way, then you must include this tool in your toolbox. A Twitter page adds credibility to your business.

Twitter is a social media platform where members converse in 140-character messages called "tweets" via the Twitter website, as well as cell phones, email, IM, and even Facebook. You create conversations or you join them. You follow people who interest you, and people who find you interesting follow you. Following (and unfollowing) is completely dynamic, much like in-person conversations at a networking event or party. To create cash, you will want loyal followers. You can create loyal followers by following people you like and trust, and who dominate a niche similar to the one you are creating.

Let's get started with the step-by-step process:

1. **Create your account.** If you don't have an account yet, go to Twitter.com and click on sign up now. If you already have an account, ensure you have the following items.

- Add a photo of yourself to your profile, preferably just your face, with a smile on it. You know how you feel when someone genuinely smiles at you. You want people to feel the same about you.

- For the web address, insert the address to your webpage or marketing site. A link to your blog or video blog is best.

- Unless you live off planet, enter something real for your location.

- Create a bio that says something about you or what you do in 160 characters or less.

All of these items are important for creating a set of reference points that enable people to identify with and connect to you. Not only do first impressions count in this medium, the first impression may be all you get. Twitter is immediate, and Twitter users will not wait around while you are designing the perfect bio and posing for the professional headshot. When someone follows me, I look first for their profile photograph, then their web address. I also look for their latest tweets. If any of these are absent, or their tweets are only about getting the greatest number of followers, or only about them or their product, then they are probably spammers, or not your target audience.

A creative background is great for getting you noticed, but is only window dressing if you don't have the other items in place. Get Twitter working well for one income stream before starting a new one. Unlike Facebook or other social media, you can have many different accounts.

2. **Connect, connect, connect.** Invite your friends to follow you. Add your existing business relationships. An easy tool to use is Search on Twitter.com. Give it permission to use your contact list from your email accounts. It will present the list so you can decide whom to invite. If you are already in other social media, such as MySpace, Facebook, LinkedIn, Plaxo, Ecademy and others, you can invite people already linked to you to follow you on Twitter. There are many tools to increase the number of followers, but beware, most of those tools won't get you the type of followers that will bring you business, unless you are in the business of getting paid to generate lists of spammers and looky-loos.

Twitter has a limit of 2000 people you may follow. It is the intention of Twitter's creators you use this medium to create and develop quality relationships numbering 150-200. I have not found this number to be realistic for generating business, however, this may change with their new list functionality (more about that later). Past the 2000 limit, you may still follow people, but at a reduced rate of not more than 120% of the number of people following you. The key to this metric is to create as many reciprocal relationships as possible: *You follow me and I follow you, because we both believe we will benefit from the relationship.* Before reaching the 2000 limit, you could still be halted by Twitter, if it appears you are massively following others without them following you back. This could get you labeled a spammer, and your account could be locked out. So proceed with caution and deliberation.

3. **Start tweeting.** Share in 140 characters what you are doing, have done or are going to do; information or a link that can be valuable to your followers; an inspiring quotation; or simply ask a question. Share cool stuff your followers will like. The key is variety.

4. Get quality followers. Here are some tactics for your tweeting strategy to create quality followers:

- **Get tweeted about.** If you are interesting and genuinely interested, others will tweet about you.

- **Retweet others.** This is known as RT for retweet. If you like what someone says, or find a link they've posted interesting, by all means retweet it to others. Your followers may find it interesting. You may be publicly thanked by the original tweeter. Remember to thank those who retweet what you've tweeted. Use this format: RT @(name of tweeter) followed by what you are retweeting. There is also a retweet button that looks like a gray recycle symbol that becomes visible when you hover your mouse over a person's tweet. Sometimes, something is popular enough that a number of people have retweeted it already. If you still wish to retweet, remove all but the original @tweeter to still give proper credit.

- **Share pithy statements or information items of interest to you.** You will attract people who share tastes and ideas similar to yours. These people are more likely to be interested in what you have to sell, or will know someone else who is. It is okay to tweet the same message once in a while.

- **Tweet sparingly about your product or service.** Lean toward inviting people to subscribe to your blog or better yet, your video blog. Video excites most people's attention, and they will click on one out of curiosity.

- **Create a fundraiser for your favorite charity or cause, and invite others to join.** Be sure to set a deadline. An outstanding example of this was when Ashton Kutcher (@aplusk) decided to be the first to get a million

followers, and in so doing, raised both funds and awareness about Malaria No More!'s mission to eliminate
malaria in the world (@malarianomore). Another excellent example of this was @DeniseWakeman's contest to
raise $5000 for Kiva.org for her 50th birthday, in which
I participated. Not only did I get to know Denise better,
but I met more interesting people in the same cause.
When I decide to run a similar fundraiser, she has already pledged to support me by contributing funds and
retweeting my efforts.

- **Create a contest.** People love to win and will eagerly sign
  up if you have interesting prizes. I won a hand-poured
  Key Lime Pie scented soy candle from a company named
  Things That Make Scents by way of @LaughTub, who gen-
  erates daily and weekly humor to promote his websites
  and his affiliate websites.

- **Follow well-known tweeters,** particularly those who are
  in your industry or your target market

- **Use hashtags** to follow people in your target market.
  Engage them in a dialogue, but do not try to sell them.
  Hashtags are like tags added inline to your post. They
  add additional context and metadata to your tweets.
  You create a hashtag simply by prefixing a word with a
  hash symbol: #hashtag. Used sparingly and respectfully,
  hashtags can provide useful context and cues for recall.
  Don't use it excessively, because people will stop following you if you annoy them. Only use hashtags when they
  add value, rather than on every word in an update. Start
  using hashtags in your tweets, preceding key words. It is
  best to do a little research first, to find out if the subject
  you're tweeting already has an established hashtag.

- **Thank people for following you.** Take time to visit their

Twitter page and if possible, retweet something from there. This will cause them to notice you as you begin to build your reputation as a team player and helpful person.

- **Twitter Lists.** You may create lists of your own, and make them public or private. This allows you to organize your followers and watch streams of only their tweets. If your list is public, others may subscribe to your list. It makes grabbing followers for the sake of large numbers obsolete as you may add someone to your list without actually following them. Create one of your lists to include the leaders of your industry, and add their top followers. Not only can you learn from whatever they are tweeting about, you can retweet useful items of information to your followers.

- **Gather information about your industry, product, service, and competitors.** This is often an overlooked tool. Twitter is a treasure trove of up-to-the-moment information. Type a word or phrase or even your own business in the "Search" box on the right hand side of your Twitter home page and click on the magnifying glass. This allows you to see conversations and comments in real-time. This is better than a party, because you can look in on conversations before deciding to join.

5. **Grow your database.** Ask people guiding questions to determine what they need. When you tweet about what you have to offer, invite people to your website to learn more. Once there, invite them to sign up for your free newsletter, or to subscribe to free feeds of your blog. People love free things, especially useful information. Now you can use both your newsletter and your tweets to build your database. This is where your gold lies.

6. **Build credibility.** These days, the most successful authors, speakers, show producers, and writers are successful because they are inviting their audience to participate in the creation process. Create a list of the best people in your industry, and retweet their information to your followers. By borrowing off the credibility of those more successful than you, you are building your own credibility. People know they can trust you, because they know if you don't have what they need, you know who does, and can refer them. Not only will the leaders thank you, they will engage you in mutually profitable ways.

7. **Track for customer service and listen, listen, listen.** Comcast was known for unfriendly customer service. Under the Twitter name of comcastcares, the company's Senior Director of National Customer Service didn't tweet about the benefits of Comcast; instead, he began actively listening and responding to what consumers had to say. You can do the same. Listen to what your customers or clients have to say. Their feedback can help you improve your product or service.

8. **Create strategies and track your results.** For example, use a service such as bitly.com to shrink the links you post. Bitly is useful because you can track the number of hits to your site via your contracted link. This can assist you in determining how well your strategy is working.

9. **Have fun! Make money!** The potential is limitless.

Twitter works as well as it does because we have made the shift from pushing data onto people to interacting with them. Transparency is also part of this new shift in our culture. Companies have literally changed customers' perceptions of them overnight using Twitter like Comcast did.

An often overlooked aspect of Twitter is access to other's

databases. Get the Twitter name of your customers or somebody you have done business with, and tweet your positive experiences about them, being sure to include their Twitter name. They will retweet your comments to their followers along with your Twitter name, thus bringing more interest to you. This is a mutually winning situation you will want to take advantage of, as long as both of you are sincere in your comments.

As with any method of communicating on the Internet, be safe and discreet. While you are certainly branding yourself and getting noticed all over the world, remember there are those who will take advantage of your information and steal your identity if possible. Also, be appropriate about what you say, and what information you pass on. What gets put on the Internet will always be there, as long as the Internet continues to exist. Every tweet you make is stored forever and can be accessed any time in the future.

Be aware of your time. A pitfall for many is distractibility. There are many interesting tidbits of information, and the ability exists to dive deep into a topic of interest, or to skitter from one interesting conversation to another. It is not unusual for someone to resurface after many hours, feeling exhausted and irritated because they didn't accomplish anything, and their head hurts from an overload of useless detritus. It is helpful to tweet a few times a day, but don't overdo it.

There is an incredible set of tools available to you to enhance your basic experience as well as take advantage of the more advanced features. Some features are offered by the Twitter Team, many more are offered by the users themselves. Many are free, some of these ask for a donation, and some of the more advanced features are available to purchase. Some of the ones I have found useful are: Hootsuite, Tweetdeck, Seesmic, and Tweetie. I also like Tweepi.com for intelligently choosing to follow or unfollow those who have not followed me back. As this is a rapidly shifting landscape, listen to what others say. New tools are arriving all the time. On your Twitter home page, for example, you will see some of these in the right hand column, looking something like an entry in the dictionary. It is also a live link to a blog that describes the tool.

There are those who strongly advocate automating your tweets using a tool such as Socialoomph.com. I'm not one of them. I prefer tweeting in real-time. As I expand my operations around the world, I may change my mind. I also do not recommend auto DMs (Direct Messages). A Direct Message is a tweet directed only to a person, not the public stream. Spammers and Bots have given auto DMs a bad name, so many people won't even respond to a DM. You can only send a direct message to someone who is following you. You will see this option in the far right column of their Twitter page, if they accept DMs, under Message <person's name>.

Also, there are wonderfully knowledgeable people on Twitter. My favorites are Mashable, MariSmith, Teresa Clark of Very Direct Marketing, Chris Brogan, Nathan Hangen, Robert Scoble, and Kim Sherrell, to name a few. You can follow them on Twitter to continue your learning process.

Twitter, Facebook, LinkedIn, etc. are great tools for staying in touch online; and emails are a quick way to communicate whether it is with your clients, your daughter upstairs, or somebody on the other side of the world. But when is the last time you received a card in the mail? Do something unexpected — make someone's day and send a personal card. I believe in offline marketing just as strongly as online marketing. That is why I use a powerful system of sending thoughtful and heartfelt messages in the physical form of a mailed card. The company I represent, SendOutCards, makes this easy, affordable, and unique. From any Internet connection in the world, you can send a card in your own handwriting and even include digital photos. With SendOutCards, you don't have to walk up and down the card aisle for the perfect card or stand in line at the post office for a stamp; and it has a reminder system that never lets you forget a birthday or anniversary. Whether it is new or existing people in your network, existing or potential clients, friends or family—each one of them will enjoy the experience of knowing someone genuinely cares about them. It's all part of relationship marketing, just like Twitter is.

> A friendship can weather most things and thrive in thin soil; but it needs a little mulch of letters and phone calls and small, silly presents every so often—just to save it from drying out completely.
> — *Pam Brown*

The content of this chapter was current when the book was written. Technology continues to develop, so please visit my website for the latest information.

About the author

Terza Ekholm has been online from the very early days of the Internet.

After 18 years in the high-tech industry, she decided to become an entrepreneur. She lives in Colorado, USA, with her husband who continues to work in high-tech. They have four grown children, and seven grandchildren. She loves the outdoors, loves to read and travel, and looks forward to an exciting and profitable future. Follow her on Twitter and become her fan on Facebook @TheTerzaFactor.

The best of two worlds:
how to synergize online and offline marketing

Jacqueline McCarthy

As you have been reading about Facebook and Twitter, you may be wondering, "Are the 'traditional ways' of marketing useless?" or "How can I best promote my business in this changing market place?" Good questions, and believe me, you are not the only one struggling to figure it out. The world is clearly evolving and the way products and services are being marketed today has changed. The secret is to use the best of both worlds. Jackie McCarthy is a networking expert and she will show you how to accelerate business growth and put more cash in your pocket by synergizing your online and offline marketing —

— Shamayah

The ability to form friendship, to make people believe in you and trust you, is one of the few fundamental qualities of success.
—*John J. Meguirk*

At first sight it may look complicated to synergize online and offline marketing, but if you look a little deeper, you will find there is a clear resemblance. Before we go into that, it's helpful to remember our marketing must be effective regardless of who we are marketing to. To be effective, we must tailor our marketing method to the target group we want to reach. One way to break our prospects down into different segments is by age groups. We find different age groups (generations) respond to different types of marketing strategies. As you review the generations below, ask yourself: What are their interests? How do they think? What are their values? How do they communicate?

The Forgotten Generation or Traditionalists (born in the period 1935–1945) value traditional morals, safety, and security. Conformity, commitment, and consistency are important to them. They prefer brick-and-mortar educational institutions and traditional lecture formats to online, web-based education. In the legal workplace, they favor conventional business models and a top-down chain of command. This generation is generally technologically-challenged.

The Baby Boomers (born in the period 1945–1964) are retired or heading for retirement. They are starting to sell off their big house and are restructuring their lives now that the kids are off to college and have left the nest. They like to travel and are into healthy lifestyles. If you want to connect with this generation, think about the places where you can find them. Radio, websites, and e-mails are good ways to communicate with this generation, but magazines that have their interest are also great to advertise in. Even though they were brought up to believe you work until you are 65, they are still fully engaged in life. Many are starting their own businesses.

Generation X (born in the period 1965–1994) grew up in an era of two-income families, rising divorce rates, and a faltering economy. Women were joining the workforce in large numbers, spawning an age of "latch-key" children. As a result, Generation X is independent, resourceful, and self-sufficient. This generation is comfortable using PDAs, cell phones, smart phones, e-mail, laptops, BlackBerrys, and other technologies.

Generation Y (Born in the period 1994–2009) had a cell phone before they could walk, texting their parents they were hungry ;-) This generation is very comfortable with all the widgets on their cell phone, iPods, and online learning forums — and they are often logged in 24/7.

Your target market is likely more specific than the generations mentioned above, but this basic understanding can guide you in choosing the right approach. If you are one of the baby boomers feeling overwhelmed by technology and Internet marketing, you can sit back and relax once you see that, in essence, it is the same as what you have been doing for years.

Where do you start? Well, by being an active member of your community, people will come to know you, like you, and trust you. This makes the next step — to buy from you — much easier. This principle applies to both the online and the offline world. We build relationships online in Yahoo Groups, forums, Facebook, and LinkedIn. In the offline world, we go out and meet people.

How to be a successful social networker?

Networking can be a lot of fun — if you do it the right way! You can join a local networking group, attend the Chamber of Commerce or Rotary club, or you can find a Meetup Group that shares your interest. You can also join a Business Networking International (BNI) Chapter. BNI chapters meet each week for the specific purpose of exchanging business referrals. Remember, the purpose is to help each other and not to get immediate gains. The key is not just the number of people in your network or, as with Twitter, the number of followers—it is the *quality* of the people!

Whether you meet in person or online, if you apply the following tips, you will be successful in building relationships and business:

- **Be yourself. Be genuinely and sincerely interested in the other person.** People will sense this. Networking events are to qualify potential clients. Ask questions about them and you will find out everything you need to know. This is the perfect way to qualify a person and determine if they are a potential client. Remember to turn off the WIIFM (What's in it for me?) radio station in your head. The more talking you let the other person do, the more information you will have about them and their needs. This allows you to quickly determine if your product/service is possibly a solution to their problem. Online, the same rules apply. If you join a group or a forum, "listen" to what others are saying. Focus on giving, offering suggestions, and being involved.

- **Be a professional and wait for the right moment to offer your expertise.** If you are at an in-person event, this means you only provide your business card when asked for it. Believe me, it will happen. (When you prematurely pass your card out, you are selling: when asked for it, the person is buying: this will separate you from the 95% of other people at the event and will have everyone gravitating to you at future events...) In the same way, you don't want to tweet your website all the time—it shows you are only interested in yourself and what you can sell.

- **Stay in touch.** It takes at least 6–8 contacts before someone feels connected to you and possibly wants to do business with you. For example, you can invite people you meet online or offline to join you for a networking event the following week. Create synergy by using your online social network to make the 6-8 contacts faster if you have met somebody at a local chamber event. Or, if someone you just met at a local business event tweeted a few days ago about his dog falling ill, why not break the ice in a great way by asking, "How's your dog feeling?"

♦ **Use the power of team networking.** When Kathia says that Nohra's video marketing is great, it will have much more impact on a potential client than when Nohra says it herself. You can apply this technique at local events (i.e., have others talk about your business), and you can also make an effort to find contacts on LinkedIn (or even your existing clients) who are willing to refer you by telling others about your product or service.

> People don't care how much you know until they know how much you care.
> — *John C. Maxwell*

How do you build a strong network?

1. **Be a leader.** You can start a group with one of the social networks online and you can take a leadership role in an activity or project in your local community. People will see that you care about your community and the people in it. By contributing and affecting their emotions, you have a powerful ally on your side of the court. An example of the human spirit at work is a Habit for Humanity project. You are doing something good in the community and are involving other business owners, builders, plumbers, electricians, real estate agents, local retailers, etc. Extreme Makeover: Home Edition has taken this to the extreme. Millions of

people across the nation love this show. Just imagine how effective an initiative like this will be in your local community. People love to spread the love, just give them a reason.

2. **Become an expert by writing articles.** Let the articles you write show you really care and want to help people with your expertise — free of charge. Local publications and professional journals are always looking for good content. This creates a win/win situation — you add value for their readers and they give you the unique opportunity to reach a targeted consumer group through an educational approach and the opportunity to set yourself apart from your competitors. The fun part is that you can submit the same article to ezinearticle.com and other article directories. Include your bio and a link to your website — writing and submitting articles is a great way to get readership and traffic to your website, and you are giving permission for others to reproduce your article in its entirety. "How To" articles are the most effective. People like to read your articles if you show them how to do something or what to look for while making a decision. You have now become the solution to their problem. When performed properly, writing and submitting articles will be successful. This method may take a bit more time, but it has real staying power. And remember, you don't necessarily have to write the articles yourself. In chapter 15, Peter and Dianne Ivett explain how you can find the right person to do this for you.

3. **Use the #1 marketing tool.** The most powerful marketing tool of all time is, and probably will always be, word of mouth. Do you remember the rumor mill when you were in high school? Talk about a wild fire spreading. Let's bring this analogy back to business: a friend telling you about his outrageous copywriter who increased the sales from

his website has much more impact than any other form of advertising. You trust your friend, so now you are likely to trust his copywriter. Use this same marketing tool online and have your friends and colleagues send out an email to their database for you with a testimonial or a message you would like to get out into the community. When you send out an email or a tweet, make it interesting, hilarious, and inspiring. Make it buzz worthy. At the bottom you can have your link to your website and add "Forward this message to your friends" or "Pass the word."

4. **Discover the power of the press.** Inviting the local press to an unveiling ceremony can create immense publicity. Keep in mind that this is not a "press conference." Press conferences are tricky at best and often unsuccessful at attracting the press. An unveiling ceremony is a community event and as such, residents and business owners should be invited to attend. This approach lends a better angle to the story, which in turn does a better job of attracting the media's attention.

5. **Host a Blogtalk radio show or get invited as a guest.** Setting up your own radio show is very easy with BlogTalkRadio. com. It is a web based platform that gives anyone the ability to host a live Internet Talk Radio Show, simply by using a telephone and a computer. When you host a radio show about current issues going on in your area of expertise, let people call in and ask you questions. You will become their trusted advisor. This gives credibility and legitimacy to what you're selling. People typically believe what they see in the news or hear on the radio and this will build in a trust factor that validates your claims. You can invite other business owners in the area as a guest, giving them the opportunity to be a trusted advisor (and this is also a great way for you

to build relationships). In addition, you can connect with other hosts and ask to be a guest on their show or volunteer to be a guest host should they need someone to fill in. If you are a guest, make sure you identify engaging, talkative questions that can be asked of you and forward those in advance to your host. Go ahead and push the limit or be a little controversial. When hosting your own radio show, be entertaining. Challenge people and make it interesting. Of course, you can also approach radio stations to be interviewed. Did you know that American radio stations need more than 10,000 guests per day to fill their show?

6. **Advertise locally.** When you advertise your business locally, you want to use both legs, online and offline marketing — you will run much faster! You can choose to set up a Google Adwords campaign that will only show up in your area. You can also take advantage of online directories. The Yellow pages used to be the reference book to find a product or service. Now we wonder how people ever managed to find something without Google. Make sure your website is listed with Yellow Pages and see if you can find local directories or directories for your industry where you can be listed.

Despite the fast growth of the Internet, local "printed" advertising is still a powerful way to get more customers in the door. There are many different options. How do you determine what is best for you? The average consumer is willing to drive two miles toward and one mile away from town in order to buy at any particular store. No one is willing to drive past five drugstores, for example, to get to the sixth, so pay attention to where your ad will be delivered. If you are advertising in a magazine, keep your target market in mind (i.e., the readers you wish to reach should find some value in the magazine you chose for your ad). Your ad can be delivered to 25,000 households, but it won't serve you if the magazine, with your ad, is considered junk mail and hitting the trash before it gets into the door.

One form of local print advertising that has been very effective for many business owners is Coffee News, a weekly publication filled with fun facts, trivia, jokes, horoscopes and upbeat good news stories. The huge advantage of advertising in a publication like this is that people enjoy reading it while they may be having a drink in a coffee shop or visiting a restaurant, hair salon, or any other business place where they have to wait (such as a doctor's office). Plus, it's local and flexible — you can change your ad every week. It is also exclusive — you may be the only business in your category. And finally, it's fresh — every week there is new content and the ads are rotated, and you get great results for the dollars spent.

> How can you go wrong when you are spreading good news and love?
> —*Bill Buckley, President Coffee News USA*

Keep in mind, though, that just as a perfect shape will not result from going to the gym once, one ad will not grow your business. Repetition is the key word for success. If you use your complete advertising budget on one big ad, you are wasting your money. It's much better to choose an inexpensive publication that allows your business to have the continuous, repetitive ad exposure that establishes recognition and drives sales.

About the author

Jacqueline McCarthy is a Principal of Successful Lives LLC and holds the license to publish and distribute Coffee News in Massachusetts. She has been an Associate with Winfree Business Growth Advisors, where she has helped clients achieve a threefold increase in sales. Jackie was also the BNI Assistant Director in the SE Mass/RI Region for several years. Find more Advertising, Networking, and Fun 'n Business Tips and Facts at www.coffeenewsmass. com/coffeefax.html or contact her at Jackie@CoffeeNewsMass.com.

Use Meetup.com
to attract clients

Kerrie Espuga

Meetup.com is a very effective tool for increasing your profits. In the previous chapter, Jacqueline McCarthy talked about the synergy of online and offline marketing. In this chapter, Kerrie Espuga will teach you step-by-step how you can create that synergy with Meetup. com to grow your database and build your business. She will show you where to find your target market online and how to turn those prospects into local clients. What's more, if you apply her success strategies your local presentations will come to life, making your audience want to come back for more —

— Shamayah

> The moment we begin to fear the opinions of others and hesitate to tell the truth that is in us, and from motives of policy are silent when we should speak, the divine floods of light and life no longer flow into our souls.
>
> *— Elizabeth Cady Stanton*

There I was sitting at yet another meeting in corporate America: same old topics, same old discussions, with the same people. These thoughts crossed my mind repeatedly:

♦ There has to be more to life than sitting through meetings all day

♦ I really should be following my passion for a living

♦ I know I should be making more of an impact in this world

Ever wonder what you were put on this planet to do? Ever imagine making as much profit as possible so you can spend time doing what you enjoy? Imagine six months from now, when all the hard work of your small, individual wins results in more and more substantial wins ... and there is this "never-before felt" confidence of knowing you are on the right path to success! If you see that vision and feel those benefits, you are halfway there!

As I contemplated leaving corporate America, I thought, "What's hot today? What will be hot tomorrow?" No matter where I turned or what I read, the answer was the same: "Web, Web, and Web." Then I thought, "Wait a minute ... how can I find prospects on the web, let alone make money on the web, when all I know how to do is search on the Internet and buy on eBay?" I had always been successful in Corporate America and I thought, "How hard could it be? I will figure it out." Knowing that most businesses fail within the first two years, I wanted to be well prepared to succeed. Where would I find my clients? That is when I discovered Meetup.com — a website where I could find my target market.

Since the Internet has dehumanized some aspects of communicating, the mission of Meetup.com is to connect people online with the goal of connecting them in person at a local Meetup group. Did you know Meetup.com already has a database of local people interested in hundreds of topics? Whether you are targeting small business owners or individuals, chances are, they have entered which topics interest them most on Meetup.com. Then, when an organizer (you, in this example) creates a Meetup group for that person's interest, that person will be notified! It is that simple! You get instant access to the database of interested prospects. Would you like to learn how to find your target market online and turn those prospects into local clients? Keep on reading.

Meetup.com logistics

Meetup organizer set-up

Decide on a topic (e.g. your business) for your local Meetup group. Go to Meetup.com and search for that particular topic in your area. There are two reasons you want to do this: First to see your competition's approach and second, to find out how many of those groups already exist. Is the local market saturated with many groups on this topic, which would dilute attendance at your meetings? Sometimes forming a partnership is a better idea. On the flip side, perhaps no "Organizer" has begun this particular kind of group yet. Is that due to no demand (failed attempts) or because nobody has ever taken the initiative to form a group in your business niche? It could be a strong leader was needed to keep the group active.

Regardless, if all looks good, create an account. Sign up as an "Organizer." After you set up a group, Meetup.com will automatically ask if you would like an announcement to be sent to all Meetup members who have shown interest in your topic. With one click, local interested members are notified of the new group and then they can choose to join and/or RSVP for your first event. That is the best part about Meetup.com. They already have the targeted people waiting for groups to start. Take advantage of their database! Also, take advantage of the Organizer's forum to learn best practices. There is no need to reinvent the wheel. Learn from others who have been running successful events.

Meetup fees

The fee for the Organizer is nominal and includes the ability to create 1-3 groups. After signing up as an Organizer follow all the prompts to make your group's page stand out to attract Members: use a creative name and a creative background (e.g., photo); set up your first event, and choose a venue (venue ratings are available on Meetup.com). Choose a fee for Members to attend your event. I would highly recommend charging a fee for admittance. My first event only had one person since it was free. Ever since that failed attempt, I have been charging $10-$50 per meeting and members pay in advance. Think of this charge as a small first step in building them into loyal clients (i.e., this is the top of the marketing funnel you read about in chapter 5). Another added advantage is I don't worry about attendance: when people pay in advance, they feel more committed to attend. If it is free, they do not feel obligated to show up. People value what they pay for.

Venue for Meetup group

Call the venue directly to reserve a room. Take into account ambient noise volume. Is it a private room? Is there a room charge? Is it convenient and close to the main highway? Confirm the day prior to your event.

Meetup member communication

Whenever someone joins, send a personalized welcome, from either you or your assistant organizer. Whenever someone RSVPs, send a personalized message. The more personal attention they get, the more excited they will be about your group, and the more likely they will RSVP. You can set up automatic events and automatic reminders. Just make sure you are not manually reminding Members at the same time as the automatic ones go out. Nobody likes "spammers."

Checklist for event logistics

♦ Assistant organizer sends reminders to all Members (those who have and have not RSVP'd).

♦ Take digital camera and video camera. Remember, chapter 7 talked about creating information products? This is a great way to create that content!

♦ On the sign-in sheet, ask for their name, email ("free e-newsletter"), and phone # ("free consultation") for next steps and to follow up later. Obtaining this info on site is critical for increased revenues later.

♦ Arrive early to set up chairs, tables, water, etc. (Arriving at the same time as Members is a sign of disorganization).

♦ Hang up Meetup signs with your topic and name, to facilitate the Members' finding you.

♦ Videotape your events. The videos can later be used to create a product, such as a link for promotion of future events, or DVD with five events in one.

♦ Always expect a few people not to show up and a few people to be late. One idea is to have an assistant who can greet the late ones. That way you will not be constantly interrupted. The assistant can also be in charge of the video camera, sign-in sheet, etc.

♦ If you have a product to sell, allow for extra time at the end. It is crucial to understand that if you provide value, participants WILL want to know next steps.

♦ Get 30-second video testimonials from people who truly appreciated the session. They will be happy to share their sentiments. Upload testimonials for promotion on your group's webpage. Upload photos as well (so those who did not attend can see what they missed and be more apt to join and attend next time). My Meetup videos have gotten about 500 views (with zero advertising dollars).

♦ Follow up with all attendees via email and better yet, call them to set up a time for a free consultation. Remind them of the next steps you want them to take. Think of this as the second step to building a lasting relationship with them as a loyal client.

Presentation strategies

Now that we know how to run a successful Meetup group, let's explore ways to captivate our members' attention so they turn into loyal clients. After all, haven't we all sat through more than enough boring meetings? Wouldn't it be great to give presentations people enjoy listening to?

Ever wonder how some speakers have so much charisma? Ever notice that people who speak eloquently have higher paying jobs? Think of successful entrepreneurs you know. Chances are, they are dynamic presenters. How are they able to speak with such influence?

Jerry Seinfeld once said 20 years ago that people would rather be in the casket at a funeral than stating the eulogy. Why is public speaking still the number one fear in the US? Is it because we are afraid the audience is judging us or that they will outwit us by asking questions we can't answer? Speaking skills are crucial for success in any business. Whether you speak in front of a group or give your "elevator pitch" to a single individual, when you become a dynamic presenter, you will make more money.

Let's explore some insider secrets to speaking with confidence.

1. **Use an outline.** People always ask, "How do I prevent freezing? How do I prevent going completely blank when I'm in front of the room? How do I remember everything that I want to say?" Remember the key points you want to share instead of having notes with full sentences. Avoid memorizing everything you want to say. Jot down a few necessary bullet points to illustrate your main points and the overall purpose of your talk, and then in front of the group, use your own words. The reason we sound natural one-on-one is because we are using our own words. Simply glance down for an idea and then speak with the audience in your own words as if you are talking to your friend.

2. **Apply feedback.** To reiterate, as in real estate, it's "location, location, location." With public speaking, it's "practice, practice, and practice." Practice your opening remarks and closing comments in front of someone and get their honest feedback. Practicing without feedback is like not practicing at all. Some speakers believe they're doing really well, but then wonder why business is not pouring in. Could it be that they need to speak with more influence? Have your friend attend your Meetup group and answer questions like, "How was my confidence in that room? Did I convey the message appropriately? Did I sound convincing? Would you have signed up as my client?" Imagine if one small tweak in your close got 10 more people to sign up? Get feedback from other Meetup.com "Organizers" by asking questions on the forum. That way you can gain insight without reinventing the wheel. You can also become a member of a local Toastmasters club. This organization has been around for more than 85 years and offers a proven and enjoyable way to practice and improve your communication skills.

3. **Improve your non-verbal communication.** Watch the faces, the appearances, and the body language of leaders. What makes his or her communication so powerful? There are several aspects to model which are all crucial to engage your audience:

 ♦ Make eye contact. Hold eye contact for a full sentence with one person in the audience. Most speakers look over participants' heads, and scan the wall, then the floor, or ceiling. Your eye contact alone, will separate you from your competitors.

 ♦ Let your face be fully animated. Use your face and your eyebrows to express emotions.

 ♦ Use large gestures with your arms to emphasize your words.

 ♦ Be dressed professionally. Does your attire align with your message? Does your "look" align with the desired image you would like to portray? If your message is about being casual, go casual. If you're speaking with boardroom executives, you might want to put on that top-notch suit.

4. **Keep your feet planted.** When your feet are still you exude confidence. Avoid pacing back and forth or doing the "cha-cha" side to side. This is perceived as nervous energy. Your audience can get distracted by your feet (and might question your confidence and credibility). Keep your feet still, and then use arm gestures. That will keep your audience engaged and focused on you and your message, instead of on your feet. This strategy will keep them connected, and you will be able to engage your audience with much more credibility. The only time your feet should be moving is if the movement is part of the story (e.g., if your story is about climbing stairs or exercising). The art of planting your feet

takes talent and practice (very few speakers do it well), so if you're just starting out, be sure to keep feet still.

5. **Make sure your voice is on par with your message.** When you are excited about your topic, your audience will be too. They can SEE your passion in your gestures and movements. They can HEAR your passion in the energy, emphasis, and inflection in your voice. If you are referring to the drop in the economy, have a serious tone. If you are talking about the benefits of your firm, smile, and discuss what CLIENTS have said about your organization. It's easier to brag about your business when using testimonials (by mentioning clients' words). Your voice should include appropriate inflection, tone and pitch.

In summary:

+ Use an outline for notes, not full sentences.

+ Apply feedback.

+ Improve your non-verbal communication.

+ Keep your feet planted

+ Make sure your voice is on par with your message.

Be sure to implement these recommendations and make your Meetup groups come to life. Soon, your Internet prospects will turn into local clients. Practice makes proficient. Imagine yourself becoming a powerful magnet attracting all the clients you desire. Learn how to captivate your audience and go to *http://www. corporatetrendsetters.com* to get your DVD on how to become a powerful speaker.

As mentioned above, Meetup.com is an effective way to meet prospects online and then meet them locally. It is much easier to turn them into clients, because they are interested in your topic. Meetup.com already has prospects just waiting to be contacted. Start with small steps for your introduction by offering them a small incentive to connect with you. What can you offer to them for free (or for a nominal fee)? What do you do well? What could you teach them? Meetup.com is an alternative way to build a following, based on the value you are offering. Then, once you have built that trust, offer the larger packages, to eventually build them into long-term clients.

Utilize resources such as Meetup.com to drive results. Take a moment and think "What is my calling?" Do you have your answer? If so, *take action now!* Instead of just going through the motions, start living. Go for it! You deserve to make that sought-after global impact by changing lives, including your own!

> Twenty years from now, you will be more disappointed by the things you didn't do than by the things you did do. So throw off the bowlines. Sail away from the safe harbor. Catch the trade winds in your sails. Explore. Dream. Discover.
>
> — *Mark Twain*

About the author

Kerrie Espuga is founder and Managing Director of Corporate Trendsetters, LLC, a New York professional training firm. She is known for her expertise in training Public Speaking and Sales/Management workshops. In the Sales arena, she won three Annual National Winner's Circle Awards and as a Sales Manager, led her team from last in the Nation to #2. Often referred to as the "Funenergetic" Trainer, she enjoys keeping groups engaged and entertained to enhance the learning! Get free public speaking tips at http://www.corporatetrendsetters.com.

# Free up time with a Virtual Assistant

Janice E. Clements

It is the weekend! Your friends have invited you to see that great Broadway Show and then have dinner at that fabulous restaurant in the city. You know the one: with the fancy linen tablecloths and the wait staff that pampers you as soon as you walk through the door. What a great way to start your weekend! But, you are going to miss it. Why? As a small business owner you have obligations to your clients, job tasks to complete, and deadlines to meet. On top of that, you need to do your own paperwork—billing, invoices, and meeting confirmations. Feeling overwhelmed? Are you asking yourself where the rewards are for being a business owner? Did you imagine being buried in your own paperwork? If this feels like you, I have good news for you! Janice E. Clements enjoys educating clients on the value of Virtual Assistants, team concepts, and team leadership; and she is here to help —

— Shamayah

> Until you value yourself,
> you won't value your time.
> Until you value your time,
> you will not do anything with it.
> — *M. Scott Peck*

A Virtual Assistant can help you with your work overload so you can concentrate on important business growth strategies such as retaining new clients, offering more services, dedicating more time to individual clients, and generating more revenue.

What is a Virtual Assistant?

Let's start with the definition: "A Virtual Assistant is an independent entrepreneur providing administrative, creative, and/ or technical services. Utilizing advanced technological modes of communication and data delivery, a professional Virtual Assistant assists clients in his/her area of expertise from his/her own office on a contractual basis."

Virtual Assistants are entrepreneurs just like you. Owning their own businesses, they work from their own offices and utilize today's technology to deliver their services and communicate with their clients. Working remotely from their client's premises, they can effectively provide the same level of service and output provided by an in-house administrator. You can hire them on an as-needed basis, or on a retainer — with a specific amount of committed hours per month. They structure their own operating standards, practices, and policies, determine their own rate, and are responsible for paying their own self-employment taxes.

What can a Virtual Assistant do?

There are a myriad of services that Virtual Assistants can provide to entrepreneurs, small businesses, not-for-profits, and many other business sectors as an outsourcing solution. Examples include managing administrative tasks, providing business and/ or technical support, conducting marketing activities, communications, customer service tasks, or specialty services.

Why hire a Virtual Assistant?

The business environment is more competitive, more global, and more demanding than ever before. By having a Virtual Assistant on your team, you can concentrate on growing your business — increasing the customer base and, ultimately, increasing the business profits. One Virtual Assistant helped her client triple his income within a year by taking care of all the time consuming tasks that didn't make him money, like answering emails and scheduling calls, so he could focus on what he does best and enjoys most.

What are the business benefits?

- ♦ **Business development.** Hiring a Virtual Assistant gives the business owner more time to concentrate on the core business, take on more work, and generate more revenue. Let someone else do the administrative tasks of typing, phone calls, billing, etc. Trying to do it all is costing you revenue, and your sanity! More free time allows for more networking, increased business contacts, and an increased customer base. More business for you! A specialty Virtual Assistant can carry out specialized tasks such as fundraising, project management, or event planning. Again, this allows you to concentrate on your core business, while executing special events for the business.

- ♦ **Cost effective.** You don't have to pay for payroll taxes, vacation pay, sick days, workers' compensation, and employee benefits such as health, dental, and insurance benefits. Once you have agreed on a charge rate, there are no other hidden rates. You pay an hourly rate and the Virtual Assistant is responsible for all other costs, which eliminates the entitlement mentality of staying on a job for the benefits. You don't have to pay an overtime premium.

* **No professional development expenses.** The Virtual Assistant has a vested interest in keeping his/her skill set current. The better the skill set, the more opportunity to attract and retain clients. A good Virtual Assistant will continue with his/her education, training, and certifications.

* **Lower your overhead.** You don't have to purchase additional office space or equipment, or invest in upgrades to computers, software, phone systems, desks, lighting, and other essential requirements that normally are needed for employees.

* **Redirect your energy.** Life can be stressful. Trying to be all things to your business, family, and friends can create an overwhelming sense of emotional and physical strain. However, with a Virtual Assistant, you can spend more time with your children — and they will enjoy it more, because you can be present with them instead of thinking about everything you still have to do. When you get back to work, you are refreshed, recharged, and more productive.

Virtual Assistants free up your time and save money and frustration.

How can I use a Virtual Assistant for my business?

This a *partial* list of business services they can provide:

Appointment Confirmations	*Mailing Services*
Answering/Voicemail Services	*Marketing and Advertising*
Bookkeeping	*Medical Billing Service*
Billing and Invoice	*Meeting Planning*
Blogging	*Newsletter Publishing*
Business Plan Writing	*PowerPoint Presentations*
Calendar Management	*Project Management*
Collection Service	*Real Estate Support*
Computer Training	*Research and Development*
Concierge Services	*Resume Writing*
Copywriting	*Sales Support*
Desktop Publishing	*Spreadsheet Design*
Email Management	*Template Creation*
Event Planning	*Transcription Services*
Graphic Design and Editing	*Travel Arrangement Services*
Language Translation	*Website Design and*
Legal and Paralegal Services	*Maintenance*

What to look for in a Virtual Assistant?

First, start with yourself. What is needed to effectively run your business? What do you need help with? Identify the tasks that are prohibiting you from growing your business. Once you clearly understand what you are looking for, you are prepared to hire a Virtual Assistant whose skill set and character match your requirements. There are two things to consider — business skills and personal traits. Hire the correct skill(s). Once you have found a potential candidate, proceed with a phone interview or one-on-one consultation. Most Virtual Assistants will provide a complementary consultation to assess business needs and determine if there is a proper fit. Remember, this is a business relationship with the goal of completing work in a timely fashion at the highest quality and professional level.

Types of questions to ask to ascertain legitimacy:

♦ Number of clients, years of service, and types of services offered

♦ What are the credentials?

♦ What is the business structure? Is it a legal entity?

♦ Does the business have the required insurance, licenses, and permits?

♦ Inquire about client names for reference checks

♦ Is a portfolio of past clients and the work performed available?

Types of questions to ask about traits:

♦ What is the requirement with regards to task lead-time, turn-around time, and rates?

♦ Are they willing to take on "emergency" tasks? How does he or she manage an "emergency request"?

♦ Is he or she willing to work with you to assist, seek understanding, and fulfill task requests? If emergency tasks are a repeat pattern, a good Virtual Assistant will help you to become more organized

A serious Virtual Assistant will have business agreements as part of her business portfolio and is willing to sign a confidentiality agreement. How the Virtual Assistant runs her own business can be an important insight into the detail and attention she will give your tasks. Of course, you want to hire somebody who is skilled, organized, trustworthy, respectful, and communicates openly and honestly. Remember, they are working for you. Make the most of your investment.

Where do I find a Virtual Assistant?

The best way is word-of-mouth. People are always willing to share their experiences. Ask small business owners, entrepreneurs, friends, and family if they can refer someone. Check out your local Chamber of Commerce and other local businesses that support business referrals. Trade journals, business groups, professional seminars, job fairs, classified ads, and websites like Elance.com and Guru.com are other ways to find a Virtual Assistant.

We are in the business of helping small businesses and entrepreneurs. Our services are sectored into three categories: administrative, social media, and specialized. Virtual Administrative Assistant (*www.myvirtualadministrativeassistant.com*) is committed and dedicated to its clients to help them succeed in business.

Very likely you will need more team members to help you grow your business. Read more about how to build your team in the next chapter.

About the author

Janice owns and operates a virtual assistant service located in New York. Her specialty is project management, event planning, and fundraising. Janice also understands the importance and value of building business relationships. She is a certified project manager (PMP) and has provided training to corporate clients in project management, process management, and software quality assurance. For more tips, information, and links, visit her website:

www.myvirtualadministrativeassistant.com. After all, we can all use a little help!

 # How to build a great team!

Peter & Dianne Ivett

How often do you say to yourself, "I am so busy" or "I don't have time?" Interestingly, you have the same amount of time as every person on the planet — 24 hours in a day. The challenge is there are so many things we want or have to do in those 24 hours. In this book you have learned many ways to grow your business online that you may now feel a bit overwhelmed and may be wondering where to find the time to implement it all. An athlete doesn't make it to the Olympics by himself. He has a team to help him perform at his best. If you want to be at your best, you cannot do everything yourself either. By building a great team you will leverage your time, capitalize on other people's knowledge and experience, and enjoy life more! Let Peter and Dianne Ivett show you how —

— Shamayah

> A team is a small number of people with complementary skills who are committed to a common purpose, set of performance goals, and approach for which they hold themselves mutually accountable.
>
> *— Jon Katzenbach*

There is a lot involved in building and running a successful business: growing your database, generating traffic for your website, setting up your video presence, creating information products for your marketing funnel, finding Joint Venture partners, networking on Facebook, Twitter and other sites, meeting new people at live networking events, being active in your community, writing articles for the local newspapers, your blog, etc., maintaining customer records, tracking sales, managing debtors and creditors, and the list goes on.

Now, pause for a moment, and ask yourself these questions:

◆ As an entrepreneur focused on building my business, is it the best use of my time to do all of these things myself?

◆ Do I have the skills and desire to do all of these things?

◆ By doing it all myself, what am I sacrificing in terms of speed to market and competitive advantage?

You need to decide if you are going to remain a one-person small business struggling to cope with all the tasks or whether you are going to build a highly successful and profitable business to take on the world, in which case you must build your team to work with you. In the end it comes down to three factors: time, cost, and quality.

◆ Time: Is this the best and highest use of your time? Do you have sufficient time or can someone with specific expertise do it faster?

◆ Cost: Do you have sufficient funds to invest to explore alternatives, educate yourself, or experiment by trial and error to get the outcome you want? If you do, why not pay someone to do it?

◆ Quality: Can you achieve the quality you require within the time and budget available? Finally, are you playing to your strengths?

Most people end up trading off one, two, or even all three of these factors; and still feel stressed and frustrated on top of that. In contrast, consider having the right team in place. The right team delivers quality outcomes that enhance competitive advantage, aids speed to market, and extracts greater value from your budget allowing you time to focus on what is important.

Where do you start in finding the right team?

People cite reasons such as trust or inability to find the right people with skills and experience for not building a team around them. To build a successful business you need the support of the right team. This means you have to discuss what you want to achieve with potential team members and understand their motivations for wanting to be part of your team.

Have clarity around these three key elements before you start building your team:

♦ **Have a Vivid Picture** — Your vision or plan paints a clear picture of what your business looks like at an agreed future point of time, at least three years from your starting point. Your Vivid Picture can feel somewhat paradoxical. On the one hand, it conveys concreteness — something visible, engaging, tangible, and believable. On the other hand, it involves a time yet unrealized — with its hopes and aspirations. If your Vivid Picture is not written, it's merely a dream. Make sure to write it down as a descriptive narrative, no bullet points. Describe in detail in the present tense the products and services you offer, who buys your offers, your pricing, what volume you sell each year, how you deal with competitors, how you develop, market and sell your products and services, and how much profit you generate. Write with passion, emotion, conviction, and commitment; and make your picture or image so real that it inspires and engages the people you want in your team.

This is what Henry Ford painted very early in the twentieth century for his bankers when asked why they should provide finance for his fledgling enterprise.

"We will build a motor car for the great multitude. It will be so low in price that no man making a good salary will be unable to own one and enjoy with his family the blessing of hours of pleasure in God's great open spaces. When we are through, everyone will be able to own one, and everyone will have one. The horse will have disappeared from our highways. In achieving this we will create the opportunity for a large number of men to be employed at good wages."

Who wouldn't want to be part of his team?

◆ **Be clear about your Core Values.** If you have not yet done so, define your Core Values. Core Values are unshakeable principles about "something" which is important to you. Often called the "deal makers" and "deal breakers," your Core Values are small in number (about five at most), simple, and easy for everyone to understand. They do not change in response to fads or trends, shift in response to changing market conditions, or allow themselves to be compromised for financial gain or short-term expediency. Core values are essential in helping you select who should be on your team. You want people on your team who share similar (but not necessarily exactly the same) Core Values with you.

As an example, let's imagine one of your Core Values is *Independence*, and someone you are considering for your team has a Core Value of *Conformity*. These Values are at odds with each other; neither of you is wrong, you simply use different values to guide your behavior. You need to know this before you begin working together, not after. When Core Values clash like the one above, it can limit potential and in some cases totally derail business ventures. As part of your due diligence, have a serious discussion with potential team members about Core Values—yours and theirs. Find a list of values on the Internet and start with those that appeal to you. Some examples are: Integrity, intuitive, co-operative, resourceful, spiritual, etc.

♦ **Have clarity on your business model.** It is pointless to search for potential team members if you can't clearly and easily explain to them the model for your business. Your business model sets out how you are going to create, deliver, and capture value. It describes your business' mission, strategies, infrastructure, organizational structures, products and/or services, trading practices, and operational processes and policies. Some examples of business models are: franchises, direct sales, multi-level marketing, online, collective resources, value-added reseller, subscription, and loyalty models.

Having clarity on your business model is important to:

- Form the basis for meaningful discussions between you and your potential team members about business growth opportunities, focus them on clarifying future direction, and address concerns they might have.

- Help ensure you get the most appropriate advice and guidance. People are not left to "second guess" what you are trying to achieve.

- Save you time and money because you are not evolving your thinking about your business on the run.

How do you determine who needs to be part of your team?

It depends on a number of factors:

* What skills and experience do you have?

* How much time do you have?

* What budget do you have?

Write down all the tasks that need to be done in your business and start creating your dream team on paper. In an ideal world, who would you like to have on your team? You may know specific people you would like to hire or you may just write down "copywriter." Once you have a complete picture, decide based on your own skills and your budget who you can hire and what you will have to do yourself for now. As your revenue grows, you can continue to outsource more and more tasks you prefer not to do yourself.

Where do you find potential team members?

There are no hard and fast rules about where you find team members. What is important is to have clarity about the skills and experience you are looking for. In addition, you must perform your own due diligence on the firm or individual you decide to use. Remember, with the power of technology, your team members can be in other cities, states, or countries. Should your financial resources not allow you to hire somebody now, your "dream team design" will at least help you to identify *potential* team members—so that by the time you can afford it, you already have a list of candidates available.

Here are some sources we have used to build our team:

- Personal recommendation/referral

- Networking Groups (e.g., Business Networking International)

- Seminars and Workshops (e.g., Live Out Loud's Cash Machine Workshop)

- Professional Associations (e.g., U.S. Internet Industry Association)

- Online and Mainstream advertising

- Chambers of Commerce

- High School and University Alumni Groups

- Telephone and Business Directories

- Community Notice Boards

How the right team helps you

Here are three stories of how the right team has helped us accelerate development of businesses in Australia. When Dianne settled on the approach for her online business she knew she needed a website. Using seminars, personal recommendations, and networking groups she realized that to have a professional website she needed specialist skills she did not have. She built an expert team, starting with a marketing strategist and a web strategist both sourced from the USA; then a website designer and builders, a social media strategist, and assistance with search engine optimization — all sourced from Australia. It took three months for Dianne to develop her team. That's relatively quick, considering she believes it saved her nine months of "trial and error" and prevented her from wasting several thousand dollars.

Our second experience demonstrates the importance of a clear business model. After a three year search we finally have a certified practicing accountant (CPA) on our team. Frustrated with our second CPA in as many years, we reflected on why we were not getting the quality of advice we were seeking. We realized it was because the CPA at the time had no interest in understanding our business or goals. One of the first questions our current CPA asked when being interviewed by us was, *"Could you explain your business model please?"* — we knew right then we'd found the right person.

The last story relates to me. After investing several thousand dollars in time and diary management programs, I went from being dreadful to just plain awful at it. I realized that scheduling is not my strength and I needed to adopt a different approach. Someone suggested a scheduling assistant. *Why didn't I think of that?* Since July 2009 I have been working with Amanda, a wonderful assistant. The results of adding this new team member are: my anxiety levels around having enough time to do things have halved; my effectiveness has improved because I'm using my time more efficiently; and business revenues have increased on average $10,000 per month — more than covering the investment in maintaining Amanda's services.

I need a team but how do I pay for it?

What if you are just starting out and resources are limited? Well, if you make $50 per hour it makes sense to hire a Virtual Assistant for $25 per hour to help you with administrative work instead of doing it yourself. You can then focus on what you love to do, and you will make more money.

On the other hand, if your budget doesn't allow for it and you have the skills to do your own search engine optimization, you may want to wait before you hire that $150 per hour Search Engine Optimization expert.

When funding is limited, start with networking and seminars to find likely team members. Yes, it means you are doing the work, but you are achieving two clear outcomes:

♦ The key to successful networking is your mindset: you are building a valued network for mutual benefit. You are not networking for what you can gain, but for what you can contribute to other network members. Using such an approach ensures you will derive valuable knowledge, as people willingly engage with people who are genuine contributors.

♦ Attend seminars that enhance existing knowledge and skills or that help close knowledge and skill gaps. Be selective and use your network to find seminars that offer value and return on your investment.

Alternatively, find a mentor who can act as a sounding board and provide initial guidance. Your mentor may be a family member or a close family friend. If funding is sufficient you may engage the services of a business coach to provide initial guidance. Visit *www.pivotal-thinking.com.au* to see an example of coaching services available.

If you need certain people on your team now but have limited funds available, first prioritize who you need and why. Do you need to employ them as an internal team member or can you purchase those services from an external provider? If you don't have the funds to pay for services, consider creative alternatives. Approaches that can motivate some people to deliver the results you require as they see the upside of sharing some of the risk with you are:

♦ Pay a small retainer plus offer an agreed upon share of profits based on success achieved

♦ Offer a bonus, the total value of which is in direct proportion to agreed targets being achieved or exceeded

Don't despair if you can't hire your dream team right away: Jeff Bezos founded Amazon.com in his garage in 1994; in 1995 Pierre Omidyar founded E-Bay in his living room in San Jose; and Larry Page and Sergey Brin brought Google to life in September

1998 when they were still students. As their businesses expanded, all of these online wizards built their team.

How do I maximize value from my team?

Let's look first at people who are employees (internal team members).

+ Have a clear role description for each person that covers:

  • The purpose of the role — why the job exists

  • The key results areas

  • The activities involved in the role

  • How performance will be measured

  • The limits to their authority

  • The agreed performance objectives for the year

+ They need to have "some skin in the game." Some part of each team member's remuneration needs to be incentivized based on performance. It is important that any performance payment is not based just on what was achieved (the task). Any incentive needs to have a task achievement component and a people management component. By people management component we mean how well they lead and manage people and/or how well customers' needs were met.

+ All roles, agreements, and contracts need to be in writing and reviewed at least annually by both parties.

Your team may also consist of external members with whom you have entered into a relationship on a contractual basis. To maximize value from external team members, there are some hard and fast rules:

◆ Know *at the start* why you are engaging the person and what outcomes you want from the engagement. Waiting until the middle of a project to develop this information can be very costly.

◆ Irrespective of what services you are seeking, "check out" potential team members even if they are recommended to you. First and foremost, check for Core Values alignment, ensure they understand your business, and ask for references and samples of recent work. Take the time to *talk* to the people they provide as references, not just about their work and its quality. Ask what they are like to work with and what they are like under pressure.

◆ If possible, meet face-to-face with your key external team members.

◆ Whether it is a designer, an accountant, or a lawyer, provide a written brief of your requirements as this provides an agreed base on which to review work and it reduces the risk of misunderstandings or loss of valuable time and money while misunderstandings are clarified.

◆ Be honest about your budget. Often people do not provide budgets because they believe the consultant, accountant, or designer will spend the budget. It comes down to trust: if you don't trust them with your money why do you want them on your team? And, of course they will spend to your budget. Moreover, if they are any good, they will deliver outstanding value for the budget you have entrusted to them.

◆ In response to the brief you have provided, wherever possible negotiate an agreed fee before work begins. Wherever possible, avoid paying for work based on an open-ended hourly rate. If an hourly rate is the only option, cap the number of hours and insist on regular progress reviews.

♦ Put important decisions, agreements, and other communication in writing — it protects everyone involved and saves precious time and money.

Know your strengths and your limitations and prioritize who you need on your team, and when. Whether it's you and one other person, or a huge team, remember this: it is not about building a team of stars, it is about building a highly effective star team that will enable you to maximize the value and returns from your online business investment. To support you in growing your business, I have written a free article for you: "Steps to Building a Vision Statement." Please download it at *www. pivotal-thinking.com.au*.

If you want to know more about building your team, please explore:

♦ *Built to Last, The Successful Habits of Visionary Companies* by James C. Collins & Jerry I. Porras

♦ *The Millionaire Maker's Guide to Creating a Cash Machine For Life* by Loral Langemeier; or, even better, attend Loral's Cash Machine Workshop.

♦ *Developing Business Models for eBusiness* by O. Peterovic and C. Kittl

♦ *Place to Space: Migrating to eBusiness Models* by P. Weill and M. R. Vitale

♦ *The Wisdom of Teams, Creating the High Performance Organization* by Jon R. Katzenbach & D.K. Smith

About the authors

A director of Pivotal Thinking Management Services, Peter Ivett has over thirty five years experience in sales, marketing, advertising and communication, organizational development, and strategic planning. Peter has extensive managerial and leadership experience. He provides coaching and mentoring services for entrepreneurs with start-up or established businesses.  Contact him at: **peter@pivotal-thinking.com.au** *or* **+61 418 834 584** *for more details.*

Dianne Ivett has a wide range of experiences in senior marketing and sales roles in Fast Moving Consumer Goods industries. She has established and run several successful businesses in marketing and strategic management consulting. Capitalizing on her many years of experience in the wine industry, she is currently establishing her own online business in this field and has experienced firsthand all of the challenges, opportunities, joys, and frustrations written about in this article! Contact Dianne at **dianne@pivotal-thinking.com.au** *or call* **+61 419 239 886** *for more details.*

Protect your most valuable asset

Theresa Giampapa

The purpose of every business is to make a profit. In this book experts have shared with you their insights on how you can use the Internet to create leverage — allowing you to acquire more time, money, and joy in life! To live by design means more than that though, because it doesn't matter how fantastic your business is going — if your doctor tells you tomorrow that you only have a few more months to live, you suddenly have a completely different perspective on your life and your business. We often don't pay attention to the subtle hints. Why wait until it's too late? Theresa Giampapa will show you how you can make little changes every day that will lead you on the road to optimal health and well-being. As a small business owner you are the CEO of your company, the CFO, the CIO, and much more. You are the central, supporting spine of your company, so taking care of yourself is the highest priority for you and your business — you are your most valuable asset! —

— Shamayah

> Take care of your body with steadfast fidelity. The soul must see through these eyes alone, and if they are dim, the whole world is clouded.
>
> — *Johann Wolfgang Von Goethe*

Do you sometimes feel you don't have the energy to get everything done? Do you have headaches regularly? Discomfort? These are all clues that your body is asking for attention. You could take drugs that minimize the complaints — until it gets worse. Or you can start listening to your body and make simple changes that will have a tremendous effect on how you feel. You may have great ideas and plans, but you can't follow through if you're too tired. Many people come home from work, eat, watch some TV, and go to bed. The next morning, they wake up sleepy and turn off the alarm three times ... as if that really is going to make a difference.

It's easier to say we need to keep balance in our lives than it is to consistently achieve it. Yet, if we neglect ourselves, we forfeit that wholeness in body, mind, and spirit which is essential for optimal productivity. An entrepreneur with a 9-5 schedule is a rare species. So I understand if you are saying, "I would like to take care of my health, but I'm so busy, I just don't have time." If this sounds like you, you simply can't afford not to take care of your health. Especially when you are busy, you need to make sure you can continue to function on this high level. You will be surprised how much more effective you can be by taking care of your mind, body, and spirit.

The first step is to acknowledge you are a priority and that it is possible to make empowering changes in your life. Make a commitment to take good care of yourself. Create the right mindset by letting go of your limiting beliefs that are telling you, "Don't bother, I have tried this before and it didn't work." Maybe the voice you hear tries to tell you, "My situation is different" or "I really am too busy." Challenge these beliefs to find out if they are supporting you or holding you back. To achieve the best potential within you, look for creative solutions by asking yourself, "How can I do it?" instead of telling yourself why you can't do it.

We too often put ourselves last. It's the way we are "wired." One way you can rewire yourself is to get somebody to clean, cook, and do your food shopping. You may think you can't afford it. The truth is you can't afford not to. In the time you save, you can go for a walk in the park. When you get back you will be so much more productive and have more clarity of mind.

With the above concepts in mind, let's now look at how to achieve wholeness in mind, body, and spirit.

Mind

A positive-directed mind is essential for optimal health. This may be surprising to you, but keep in mind that everything is connected. Every single thought and feeling has an effect on the chemistry of all our glands, hormones, and nervous system.

> We are the only creatures on earth who can change our biology by what we think and feel. If you want to change your body, change your awareness first.
>
> — *Deepak Chopra MD*

Masara Emoto has published several books with pictures of the "Messages from Water." His experiments consist of exposing water in glasses to different words, pictures, prayer, and music; freezing it, and then taking pictures of the crystals with microscopic photography. In his books you can see how positive words, like *love* and *joy*, create beautiful water crystals, whereas water exposed to negative words forms no crystals. Even though some claim his research is unscientific, it is fascinating to see the effect of positive energy — regardless if it is music, prayer, or words — on water. Considering that water makes up approximately 55% to 60% of the human body, ask yourself, "What am I telling my body? Am I treating myself with love and kindness, even when things don't go well?"

You may have problems, financial difficulties, or personal dramas that can cause tremendous anxiety. Just remember,

worrying doesn't help. It only hurts you. The best possible way
to deal with any and all of these troubles is to stop worrying and
instead pursue peace of mind.

Disappointments can be a challenge, yet by keeping a positive
attitude you will be better capable of dealing with it. There's an
old hymn with the lyrics, *Clear my mind, Lord, Clear my mind.*
Let my thoughts be only of the purest kind. Peace of mind leads
to incredible creativity and solutions you didn't even think of
may suddenly present themselves. A positive-directed mind will
direct you out of your maze of inadequacy, self doubt, and anxiety. In my heart-rending time of loss when anxiety, fear, and
devastation came near to me, I received incredible comfort by
accepting the circumstances rather than denying and resisting
them. When disappointment is met with acceptance, it opens
the door for peace, quietness, and clarity.

> Be anxious for nothing, but in everything by prayer
> and supplication with thanksgiving let your requests
> be made known to God.
> And the peace of God, which surpasses all
> comprehension, shall guard your hearts and
> your minds in Christ Jesus.
> *— Phil 4:6,7*

Body

Unless we are having serious complaints, we often take our body
for granted. Think for a moment about the marvelous functions
it performs — isn't it amazing how our eyes capture light and colors for us to enjoy beautiful sights? Or how our ears transform
sound waves into beautiful music?

Indeed, the human body is an amazing organism. Consider,
for example, our digestion? Did you ever consider putting a soda
or juice in your car instead of gas? Everybody knows that you
would not get anywhere. Our body, however, has the ability to

adapt: even if we put in the wrong "fuel," it continues to function ... but only for a while, because sooner or later we will pay the price. It's no coincidence, therefore, that cancer, diabetes, and heart disease are rampant in our society. What can you do?

Let me share with you five simple things you can do, even if you don't have time:

1. **Deep breathing.** When we are busy or stressed, we tend to breathe more superficially. To correct this behavior, breathe deeply as often as possible. Fill your lungs consciously with fresh air and blow out completely. You will notice that you will have more clarity if there is more oxygen going to your brain, and your body will feel more energized.

2. **Drink more water.** Did you know water makes up more than half the weight of the human body? All cell and organ functions depend on water, so it's no surprise that without it, we would die in a few days. How much water do you drink on a daily basis? No, coffee, sodas and black tea don't count. Ideally you should drink half your body weight in ounces. For example, if you weigh 180 pounds you should be drinking 90 ounces of water every day. Have a bottle of water next to your bed, so you can start drinking water first thing in the morning. This is when you are most toxic and dehydrated. You can even squeeze some lemon juice in it to make it tastier—plus it alkalizes your body.

3. **Give your body the nutrients to stay healthy and happy.** Isn't your body way more valuable than your car? The difference is that your car usually stops working immediately when it has a malfunction, while your body may take several years before it starts acting up. Did you know that it's estimated eight out of the top ten causes of disease in America today are directly related to food? Food has an incredible

influence on our emotional, mental, and physical states. Eating healthy, high-quality food is one of the easiest and most powerful ways to create a better life. And we're not talking about a restricted diet where you feel you're missing out on life. Learn more about the importance of alkalizing foods and regular cleansing of your body. Get a live blood test done. Eat more organic fresh vegetables, fruits, and nuts; and cut back on the crappy processed foods like cakes, sweets, and white products. Create healthy habits: Have some almonds instead of M&M's. Take an apple instead of a donut. Eat fish a few days a week instead of red meat; or even have a meatless day. It is easy. Give it a try!

4. **Find a sport you enjoy!** It doesn't matter if it is dancing, yoga, running, or blading. Just make sure it is something you look forward to and not another thing on your "to do-list." Schedule exercise at least 2-3 times a week. To make it easy, you could start with taking a 30-minute walk twice a week — even if it is just around the block. In the beginning it may take a little effort to get yourself to do it, but once you have developed the habit, you will love it!! You will notice how great it makes you feel! Plus, you will be more productive. So instead of getting less done, you are getting more done in less time.

5. **Cut back on unhealthy addictions.** Once you have made the commitment to take care of you, decide what changes you can make to support your body. Nobody has to tell you that smoking is bad for you, right? There are many ways to help you quit. Maybe you want to start with little changes, like only drinking alcohol during the weekend or reducing the amount of coffee you drink. It may not seem a big deal, but over a period of time, it can make a huge difference.

There is another very important, yet very simple thing you can do for your body — protect it against Electromagnetic Fields (EMFs). EMFs produce a toxin (commonly known as electro pollution) that may compromise your health. Simply by using your cell phone, PDA, or Bluetooth headset, etc., you may be exposing yourself each day to this toxin. Well-known and respected experts are more concerned than ever that our growing use of these kinds of devices, especially by children, is putting our health and wellness at great risk.

An eminent British physicist, Dr Gerald Hyland, wrote in an article about the effects mobile phones can have in people: "To deny this possibility yet admit the importance of ensuring electromagnetic compatibility with electronic instruments by banning the use of mobile phones in aircraft and hospitals (a prohibition driven by concerns about non-thermal interference) seems inconsistent." In other words, if cell phones interfere with aircraft and hospital electrical equipment, even at quite a distance, how can we think they won't interfere with the electrical equipment of our brain (which is recognized as an electrical organ) when held right next to it? Recent studies suggest there is a risk, as tumors tend to occur on the same side of the head where the patient typically holds his cell phone. In children, the use of a cell phone is said to be especially dangerous. In an article in the New York Times (June 2008) three prominent neurosurgeons were quoted that they did not hold cell phones next to their ears, because they want to keep the microwave antenna away from their brain.

Even though some may dispute the danger, why take the risk? Of course, we understand as a business owner in this day and age you can't just get rid of your cell phone. The good news is, you don't have to. You can use wired earphones and a chip for your cell phone to protect your brain against EMF's.

Every aspect of one's body is critical, even the outside. For example, when I mentioned to my niece that I would be going away on a business trip, she suggested I should buy a new suit and get a personal shopper to assist me. She knows I wouldn't think about my wardrobe on my own. I set an appointment with a very fashion conscious friend and we went shopping together. Those new clothes made me feel more confident and ready to conquer the world.

Spirit

In our busy lives, there is always something that has to be done. If we don't schedule time for ourselves it is unlikely anyone will do it for us. Make a conscious choice to take time out for you! For those who believe, start your day with prayer. If you have never prayed, sit in the morning before the day gets underway. Ask, "God, if you exist please show me." Even ask Him to help you plan your day. As you become more in touch with your inner self or your spirit, you will notice it gets easier to listen to your intuition and to go with the flow of life.

> All who call on God in true faith, earnestly from the heart, will certainly be heard, and will receive what they have asked and desired.
>
> — *Martin Luther*

Enjoy Nature

Take a walk in nature, whether it's in the mountains, a forest, or at the beach. There is an energy in creation that quiets the mind and brings you in touch with yourself. Spend time in nature every week and you will notice how much more peaceful you will become.

Embrace silence or meditate

It seems there is always sound and noise around us. When you're living in the city it's seldom completely quiet. Often when we come home we turn on the radio or the television.

Welcome more silence in your life. When you're silent, great ideas can bubble up from your subconscious mind that will help you achieve your goals. Meditation is a fabulous way to become silent. Some have found it easier to meditate on the psalms in the Bible. If you feel meditation is not for you, just enjoy the silence or become quiet by prayer. Distractions and self-centered thinking interfere with the flow and inspiration. To feel love and joy every day, replace habits that create negative thoughts and feelings with trust, gratitude, and appreciation. Your immune system will be stronger when your body flows with love. If you feel hatred, guilt, fear or anger, you are undermining your immune system.

Spend time with your loved ones

When asked what is most important in their life, most people will say it is their family, their spouse, their children, or their friends. Yet if you would keep track of how they spend their time, the actual hours devoted to different activities rarely reflect that. Do you spend quality time with your children and your partner? It's the special moments we share that we'll remember and which make our life worthwhile.

How can you create more time? Delegate tasks. Get a Virtual Assistant and a team, as you have read in the previous chapters. Find somebody who can help you in and around the house. For example, I love our family get-together dinners and I value our time together; so, recently I hired a phenomenal friend who shopped and cooked for me. The family loved it. It was a typical old-fashioned Neapolitan Sunday dinner. It was so worth it. This kind of balance allows me to be my best and to enjoy the time with my family.

Be aware of thoughts or beliefs that are just excuses in disguise. Don't tell yourself "One day ..." or "Some day ..." *Now* is the best moment to take action! Decide and commit to create one new habit at a time. Even if it is just drinking more water today or scheduling a walk on the beach—do something!

As you pursue that wholeness of body, mind, and spirit bear in mind you will reach your goals if you take action. It is written, *SEEK and you shall find*—much success and joy awaits you in your entrepreneurial venture!

> To succeed... you need to find something to hold on to, something to motivate you, something to inspire you.
>
> *— Tony Dorssett*

About the author

Theresa Giampapa is committed to improving the well-being of youth — on a physical, social, emotional, and spiritual level. One of the ways she does this is by raising awareness of the danger of Electromagnetic Fields (EMFs). She is the founder of Hope Leland LLC, originally born almost a decade ago to encourage Hope in people's hearts. Even though this work was initially conducted through a weekly bible study called "One Hour of Hope," fostering hope has remained the center of her activities.

 **Tip from Shamayah!**

Make sure you get enough sleep, because this will keep your immune system strong. When you sleep your cells regenerate. Choose raw food. Stop eating several hours before you go to sleep. All of these habits allow your body to cleanse itself and rejuvenate. If you are serious about taking care of your health, get your FREE video with more great tips to feel absolutely fabulous at:

www.coauthorswanted.com/health

Take action today!
Marcy Kivi

Congratulations! It's great that you have almost finished the book. You have just placed yourself in the top tier of those individuals who are really successful. Many business owners start reading, but don't follow through. That's because change takes effort and requires you to step out of your comfort zone. To create the life you really want, you can't allow circumstances or distractions determine your actions. If you stay focused on your vision, you can make your dreams come true, no matter how big they are. Decide now to live by design, instead of by default.

To get started, it is important to clearly identify what you want your outcome to be—you have to know specifically what goals you want to achieve. For example, suppose you are a chiropractor. Do you want to build your database and use social media to get more clients for your practice? Alternatively, would you like to develop educational products for your clients and sell them online as well? Or do you want to do both? Bottom line, you have to choose your destination before you start. Along the way, perhaps you will discover you need to hire team members first to free up some time. Regardless, when you are clear on your goals it is easier to make a plan and execute it. Marcy Kivi will give you tips on how to do this. —

— Shamayah

All successful people men and women are big
dreamers. They imagine what their future could be,
ideal in every respect, and then they work every day
toward their distant vision, that goal
or purpose.

— *Brian Tracy*

You have taken the first step in moving your business and life
to the next level. Taking new steps can be a bit scary, especially
if it is in unchartered territory and requires a commitment of
your time, money, or resources. Don't let fear or inexperience
stop you from achieving the results you desire. When your self-
talk is causing you to doubt yourself, read encouraging quotes
or scriptures to stay motivated and remain encouraged. Don't
get caught up in the highs and lows that might occur. Keep
forging through the murky distractions and use your intuition
and self-discipline to stay on track. Instead of giving yourself
reasons why you can't, think of all the reasons why you can.

Having a clear vision

A clear vision will support you in making decisions that are in
alignment with that vision versus getting involved in something
that takes you in the wrong direction. If you have not already
established a vision, now is the time to do so. Loral Langemeier's
program, *Building, Leading and Protecting Your Business*, is a
great resource to get you started and to identify the gap between
where you are and where you want to be. For most readers of
this book, part of your vision may include taking action now
to start making money on the Internet.

My children and I are fortunate to live in a city surrounded by
the Sierra Nevada Mountains and we are very avid snow skiers.
I would like to take you on a little ski trip that will double as an
analogy to help you apply the strategies you've learned in this

book — strategies which may seem like an unscalable mountain to you right now (there's our first analogy).

Building on this analogy, we find making the commitment to buy our ski passes is the easy part, *but determining which mountain to buy our passes for* may require some research and involve all our input and agreement. For example, there may be others who will need to buy into your decision (skiing all by yourself is not as much fun). To move those individuals in the direction that you are thinking of taking, it is important to get their input and ideas so that when it is time to take action they are on board and ready to go.

It is no different being the leader of your business. As a leader, being committed to your next course of action is necessary for its completion and success. Whether you will be delegating to employees or subcontractors or completing these tasks yourself, without your commitment and follow through to the process there will be no drive to succeed. You will need to talk about your vision and plan. You will need to remain excited about the goal, always looking at what the intended end result will be. You need to live the dream out loud so that you will not allow the negative thoughts and people to get in your way. And, of course, you will continually be reminded of past failures; but, as you talk about what you are doing and stay committed to your goal you will overcome the negativity. Those who are not enthusiastic about the direction and plan will bring you down and prevent you from success, so be mindful to select a team that understands your direction and is as committed as you are.

> The o.nly thing worse than being blind
> is having sight but no vision.
> — *Helen Keller*

When I buy my ski passes I am committed to stay with the decision I have made to ski one particular mountain. This does not restrict me from exploring the entire mountain or even going to another mountain, but I will stay with this mountain for the entire season. This decision allows me to improve my capabilities and familiarize myself with the terrain and trails of this one particular mountain.

Similarly, as a business owner, making a financial commitment will give you the motivation to forge on and move in a positive direction toward your goal(s). This focused commitment is what allows you to get the results you desire from your investment of time and money. For example, if you decide to use video marketing to generate more leads, continue to improve that strategy before you move on to the next one.

Initiate a plan of action and get organized

From your vision, create a plan with the steps necessary to make that vision a reality. Just like you need to buy the right equipment and clothing when you go skiing, you will have to determine what kind of tools you will need. Maybe you need a better computer, a faster Internet connection, or a new video camera. We dress appropriately for the weather conditions and wear helmets to protect ourselves from any unforeseen falls. How can you protect your hard drive and/or server? Do you already have a good backup system? Accidents often happen when we least expect them, and our assets must be protected.

Deciding which lifts to go up on and what part of the mountain to ski will depend on your combined skill set and capabilities. In your business, determine what you are capable of and who will need to be on your team to fill in the gaps so you can take your business where you want it to go. This process will mentally and physically challenge you, and it is likely you will learn from your mistakes and those of others. When I first started skiing, I can remember going down those intermediate and advanced runs for the first time. I couldn't even count the number of times I would fall; only to get back up and point those skis downhill again. Many times I would have to count on a more experienced skier to guide and direct me down that mountain. Let's face it—there is no other way to get to the bottom. Remember that you are not the first person or company to take this path, so seek out others who have experienced this challenge and learn from them.

You have clearly made the decision to take advantage of the Internet—after all, you have made it to the last chapter of this book. Creating the magical pages of content on your website that will capture the attention of your audience and call them to action is a critical step to forging your path. I view this as a map of the mountain. In other words, how can you possibly know which runs you want to ski on the mountain if you don't have a clear understanding of where you are and which runs are appropriate for you based on your skill level? And aren't we always looking for new challenges? As the map to your business, your website should be easy to read and navigate with useful and uncluttered information. If it is too complicated or is full of errors, then people will get discouraged and will leave before your story is told. You want to make the first impression a good one so that your potential client will stay with you. Your website should also be updated with fresh content and ideas regularly so that the search engines will constantly scan it for good placement. As Kathy Alice Brown explained in chapter 2, your website should be welcoming and engaging and establish you as the expert—someone that people will feel safe and confident following down the mountain.

Execute the plan

Executing the plan even as you are formulating it will help you weed out the things that won't work or are not applicable. Don't think you need to have the plan all figured out to get into action; even if you have to break each step down into baby steps, this is better than not making any steps at all. As long as you are doing something to move toward your goals, then you will eventually get there. Often one step will flow into the next and will not require forethought.

When you are standing at the top of the mountain looking down at the terrain below, it is imperative to formulate a course of action and push off from the edge. Once you build momentum and begin turning around and over the large moguls or mounds of snow, you may not necessarily take the exact path to the bottom of the slope that you had planned from the top; but you will still get there. Along the way you always want to instinctively stop to reevaluate the path you are on and the direction in which you wish to go. You will practice your form, speed, and accuracy; and redirect if necessary.

When we accomplish the goal, whether we achieve complete success or not, at least we can look back up the mountain completely spent, exhausted, and exhilarated and say *"I did it! Let's go again!"*

> Some people dream of success while others wake up and work hard at it.

First Impressions Business Solutions is dedicated to providing individuals and businesses highly effective and professional documents that can be used to market and advance their career opportunities. Products include: professional resumes; curriculum vitae; and professional biographies. For more information on how you can DRIVE into action, visit my website at *www. careerrevelations.com* to download a free report.

About the author

Marcy Kivi grew up in a household with six children and has learned to adapt in a constantly changing environment. She has created success by being persistent and approaching life from different directions when she didn't initially achieve the results she expected. She is creative, decisive, and professional. Marcy has spent 25 years in the corporate world of Retail, Hospitality, and Human Resources where she created marketing plans, budgets, and forecasts. Her experience managing others provided a strong background for her Professional Resume services and Business Solutions technologies. She cares about meeting the needs of her clients and helping others achieve success.

> You are not here merely to make a living. You are here in order to enable the world to live more amply, with greater vision, with a finer spirit of hope and achievement. You are here to enrich the world, and you impoverish yourself if you forget the errand.
>
> — *Woodrow Wilson*

 **Tip from Shamayah!**

When you want to learn advanced Internet marketing strategies from one of the top Internet marketers in the industry, go to:
www.coauthorswanted.com/internetmarketing.
Tom Antion is my own personal mentor and he absolutely knows how to make a lot of money on the Internet.

 # Glossary

All truths are easy to understand once
they are discovered; the point is to discover them.
— *Galileo Galilei*

Term	Definition
3G	3G is the third generation of telecommunication hardware standards and general technology for mobile networking. It operates at a higher bandwidth, giving a fuller user experience over mobile phone experiences, e.g., the iPhone.
archive	A repository for previously recorded media or documents
article-based sites	Online repositories for articles written by subscribers for subscribers in a number of different categories. Peer reviews and ratings are available.
auto responder	A computer program that automatically answers e-mail sent to it.
backlinks	Links from other pages that refer back to your page; the number of backlinks to a website is beneficial to search engine optimization.
blog	Contraction of the words "web log"—an online medium used to record experiences, observations, and adventures.

Term	Definition
Boxee	A cross-platform freeware media centre software with a three meter user interface and social networking features designed for the living-room TV.
building rapport	Developing a relationship of mutual understanding or trust and agreement between people.
bundle	A marketing strategy that involves offering several products for sale as one combined product.
buyer's remorse	An emotional condition whereby a person feels remorse or regret after a purchase. It is frequently associated with the purchase of higher value items which could be considered unnecessary
CAN-SPAM Act	On December 16, 2003, the CAN-SPAM Act established the United States' first national standards for the sending of commercial e-mail.
cloud computing	A style of computing in which dynamically scalable and often virtualized resources are provided as a service over the Internet. Users need not have knowledge of, expertise in, or control over the technology infrastructure in the "cloud" that supports them.
Content Management System (CMS)	A software platform that aids in the management of content on a website.
Cross sell	Recommending additional products or services to customers who are planning to buy something from you.
Customer Relationship Manager (CRM)	A system that maintains the processes a company uses to track and organize its contacts with its current and prospective customers.
Digital Stories	Refers to using new digital tools to help ordinary people tell their own real-life stories through the use of images or videos, married together to create a video.

Term	Definition
double opt-in	An e-mail subscription practice that requires new e-mail subscribers to confirm permission for their name to be added to an e-mail distribution list for promotions before the subscriber actually begins to receive the information.
eLearning	Learning conducted via electronic media, especially via the Internet.
e-mail campaign	One or more (marketing) e-mails sent to a group of recipients who have opted in to an e-mail list.
embedded	Video or multimedia that sits within a website, rather than having a link independent of the website.
Flickr	An image and video hosting website, web services suite, and online community platform.
future pace	The process of mentally rehearsing oneself through some future situation to help ensure that the desired outcome will occur naturally and easily.
HubPages	A website designed around sharing advertising revenue for high-quality, user-generated content.
Hulu	A website that offers commercial-supported streaming video of TV shows and movies from NBC, Fox, and many other networks and studios.
keyword	An index term, subject term, subject heading, or descriptor, in information retrieval; a term that captures the essence of the topic of a document.
lurker	In Internet culture, a person who reads discussions on a message board, newsgroup, chat room, file sharing, or other interactive system.
match	Adopting parts of another person's behavior to establish or enhance rapport.

Term	Definition
marketing funnel	Describes the pattern, plan, or actual achievement of conversion of prospects into marketing and sales, pre-enquiry, and then through the sales cycle. So-called because it includes the conversion ratio at each stage of the sales cycle, which has a funneling effect. Prospects generally enter the funnel at a lower value sale and progress to high value purchases as they pass through the funnel.
mirror	Matching portions of another person's behavior, as in a mirror image.
no-follow link	An HTML attribute value used to instruct some search engines that a hyperlink should not influence the link target's ranking in the search engine's index. It is intended to reduce the effectiveness of certain types of search engine spam, thereby improving the quality of search engine results and preventing spamdexing occurring.
on demand	Video/audio or other data that is transmitted anytime to the end-user upon request.
open-source	An approach to the design, development, and distribution of software, offering practical accessibility to a software's source code.
opt-in form	The form completed when one agrees to receive e-mails from a particular company, group of companies, or associated companies, by subscribing to an e-mail list.
organic search listings	Listings on search engine results pages that appear because of their relevance to the search terms, as opposed to their status as paid advertisements. In contrast, non-organic search results may include pay-per-click advertising.
plug-ins	A software component that adds features to another application.

Term	Definition
podcasting	A podcast is a series of digital media files, usually either digital audio or video, that are made available for download via web syndication.
poking	Poking is a feature on Facebook that can be used for a variety of things. For instance, you can poke your friends to say hello.
RSS feeds	Most commonly translated as "Really Simple Syndication" of web feed formats used to publish frequently updated works—such as blog entries, news headlines, audio, and video—in a standardized format.
scrolling or static banner	Sometimes referred to as a "marquee." A moving or static banner used on websites or video footage to give further information or for branding purposes.
search engine optimization	The process of improving the volume or quality of traffic to a website from search engines via natural (i.e., "organic" or "algorithmic") search results, based on key words, meta tags, and more.
segment	A group of people or organizations sharing one or more characteristics that cause them to have similar product and/or service needs.
social bookmarking	A method for Internet users to store, organize, search, and manage bookmarks of web pages on the Internet with the help of metadata, typically in the form of tags.
social networking	The interaction between a group of people who share a common interest in an online environment.
social networking badges	Icons or logos that are readily identified as belonging to a social networking website.

Term	Definition
spamdexing	The practice of deliberately and dishonestly manipulating search engines either to increase the likelihood of a website or page from a website being listed near the beginning of the results returned by the search engine; or to influence the category to which the page is assigned
spamming	The abuse of electronic messaging systems (including most broadcast media and digital delivery systems) to send unsolicited bulk messages indiscriminately.
Squidoo	Squidoo is a community website that allows users to create pages (called lenses) for subjects of interest.
streaming video	Multimedia that are constantly received by, and normally presented to, an end-user while being delivered by a streaming provider. The name refers to the delivery method of the medium rather than to the medium itself.
triggers	E-mail messages sent out based on actions taken by a recipient.
tweets	Text-based posts on Twitter of up to 140 characters displayed on the author's profile page and delivered to the author's subscribers who are known as followers.
up sell	A sales technique whereby a salesperson attempts to have the customer purchase more expensive items, upgrades, or other add-ons in an attempt to make a more profitable sale.
values (personal)	Beliefs of a person or social group in which they have an emotional investment (either for or against something).
viral	A video, image, or text spread by word of mouth on the Internet or by e-mail for humorous, political, or marketing purposes.

Term	Definition
viral marketing	Refers to marketing techniques that use preexisting social networks to increase brand awareness or to achieve other marketing objectives (such as product sales) through self-replicating viral processes.
Web 2.0	The second generation of the World Wide Web, especially the movement away from static web pages to dynamic and shareable content and social networking.
web conferencing	Used to conduct live meetings, training, or presentations via the Internet. In a web conference, each participant sits at his or her own computer and is connected to other participants via the Internet. This can include video as well as audio connection.
weblog	A blog. "Blog" is the contraction of the words, "web log."
wiki	A collaborative website that anyone with access to it can directly edit.
YouTube	Video sharing website on which users can upload and share videos.

The Glossary has been written by Meredith Collins.
You can find more of her valuable resources on
http://www.videosocialmarketing.net

 **Googlicious
Resources & Links**

We are here to help. If you want to learn more about the different aspects of Internet marketing, if you would like a strategy session to get you started, or if you would like to outsource your online activities, please feel free to contact us. Call 877-777-6292, email us at info@googliciousbook.com or visit *www.googliciousbook.com*.

We do more than help businesses with their online marketing strategy. We can also help you get your book written, with co-authors or without. A book is a great way to share your message or knowledge with the world. It gives you credibility and can make you the authority in your field. Please contact us at 877-777-6292, via email at info@coauthorswanted.com, or visit *www.coauthorswanted.com* to find out how we can help you grow your business by using the power of a book.

Please share your experience using *Googlicious* in your business, or give us your feedback — we would love to hear from you!

In Joy,
Shamayah Sarrucco
shamayah@googliciousbook.com

Download this page at
www.Googlicious.book.com/links

www.coauthorswanted.com/bookspecial
Become an author and grow your business

www.coauthorswanted.com/turningpoint
Improve your life through subconscious reprogramming

www.yoursuccessfulwebsite.com
Free report, "5 Ways to get your website Googlicious"

www.coauthorswanted.com/uptrends
Free 4-week trial to monitor your website. Receive reports about uptime, downtime, load time, and errors.

www.google.com/sktool
Keyword tool to do competitive research

http://seodominators.com/resources
Tools and services to automate your SEO

http://SEODominators.com
24/7 access to step-by-step SEO video tutorials

http://12seconds.tv
Tweet videos directly from your Blackberry,

http://yfrog.com
iPhone, or laptop

http://twitvid.com
www.videomarketingmakesyoumoney.com
A video presence that increases your business

www.coauthorswanted.com/videoemail
Free 30-day trial for video and audio email

www.coauthorswanted.com/stefanie
Free interview with Top Marketing Strategist

www.coauthorswanted.com/jvclub
Create powerful relationships. Join the Private Joint Venture
Club.

www.erica.lewis.com/welcome
Articles and information on various aspects of
entrepreneurship

www.earnprofitsfromyourpassion.com
Launch your entrepreneurial career using books or other information products

www.leadingfrominspiration.com
Spice up your communication

www.coauthorswanted.com/assessment
Find your own personality and behavioral style

www.videosocialmarketing.net
Free video, "How to Get Traffic with Social Media'

www.successfullives.com
Free daily "Quote to Action"

www.coffeenewsmass.com/coffeefax.html
Advertising & Networking Tips and Facts

http://highpowerpres.com/sq
Free public speaking tips

www.myvirtualadministrativeassistant.com
Virtual Assistant services

www.elance.com
Outsourcing website

www.odesk.com
Outsourcing website

www.guru.com
Outsourcing website

www.pivotal-thinking.com.au
Free article, "Steps to Building a Vision Statement"

www.hopeleland.com
Free video, "How to protect yourself against electro pollution"

www.coauthorswanted.com/health
Enjoy optimal health and longevity

www.careerrevelations.com
Free report, "How you can drive into action"

www.coauthorswanted.com/internetmarketing
Learn advanced Internet marketing secrets from the top marketer in the industry

www.coauthorswanted.com/shoppingcart
Set up your autoresponder and shoppingcart

www.coauhorswanted.com/audiorecording
Create audio recordings for your website

www.coauthorswanted.com/loral
Learn to build your own cash machine: attend Loral Langemeir's workshop

It's just me—But I am somebody. I can't change everything, but I can change something. I won't be able to save the world, but I can touch one person's life. And if each one of us touches one person, together we will make a difference.

Every day The Shade Tree changes lives ...

By providing safe shelter to homeless and abused women and children in crisis and offering life-changing services that promote stability, dignity, and self-reliance. *The Shade Tree* offers programs for women that support them to rebuild their lives: find employment, secure permanent housing, and become productive members of the community. The shelter provides immediate safety from the harshness of the streets, street crime, and domestic violence.

The Shade Tree is the largest shelter of its kind in Nevada, and is the only 24-hour accessible shelter designed specifically to meet the needs of women and children in southern Nevada. With 364 permanent beds, *The Shade Tree* provides some 80,000 nights of shelter each year.

Thank you for buying this book and contributing to the great work *The Shade Tree* does. Live by Design Books supports *The Shade Tree* by giving a percentage of the profit from *Googlicious.*

Go to *www.theshadetree.org* to touch somebody's life and make your donation.